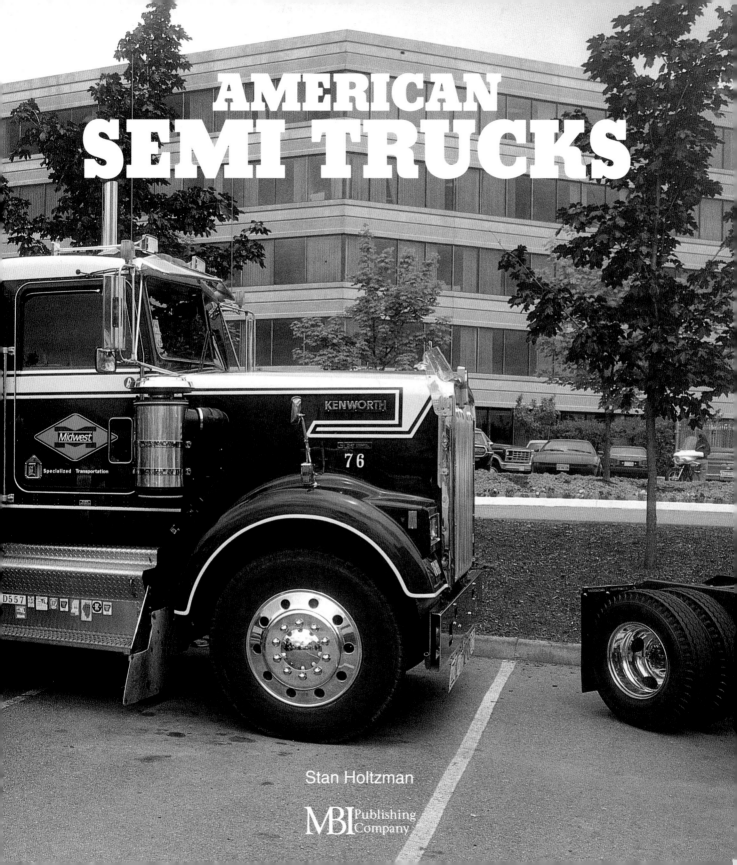

AMERICAN
SEMI TRUCKS

Stan Holtzman

MBI Publishing Company

"What I miss most about trucking in the past, was the professionalism that prevailed both with competing companies and by the truckers themselves . . . there was always time to help each other."

Gene Olson
Chairman Emeritus
American Truck Historical Society
Past CEO/Pirkle Refrigerated Lines

This edition published in 2004 by Motorbooks, an imprint of MBI Publishing Company, 400 First Avenue North, Suite 300, Minneapolis, MN 55401 USA

First publsihed in 1995 by MBI Publishing Company.

Motorbooks titles are also available at discounts in bulk quantity for industrial or sales-promotional use. For details write to Special Sales Manager at MBI Publishing Company, 400 First Avenue North, Suite 300, Minneapolis, MN 55401 USA.

To find out more about our books, visit us online at www.motorbooks.com.

ISBN 978-0-7603-2021-1

On the front cover: The late-model Marmon conventional pictured here is a favorite in the owner-operated sector of long-distance trucking. More and more "bedbug-haulers" like this one, pulling for Atlas Van Lines, are tired of owning "just another Class 8 big rig" and want something different. Marmon fills this need.

On the frontispiece: Although Roscoe Wagner is deceased, his livestock trucks live on . . . a legacy to the man who began hauling cattle in Twin Falls, Idaho, in 1935.

On the title page: A 1928 and a 1986 Kenworth. Part of a larger fleet owned by Allen Koeing and Midwest Specialized Carriers of Rochester, Minnesota.

On the back cover: Mark Bridgwater of Claremont, California, owns this 1954 model series 630 "Jimmy." It sports a 471 engine and a five and three transmission. Notice the one-piece windshield.

Printed in China

Contents

Acknowledgments

Special thanks go out to all of the truckers who allowed me to take the various photos of their rigs. Many of the truckers who have helped me are no longer with us and I will never forget those folks that have influenced my life.

Because of limited space, a lot of makes and models do not appear . . . this is certainly not an oversight on my part. This book, because of its limitations, does not attempt to go into a detailed history of each make of vehicle but rather attempts to "fast-forward" the reader and bring them up to speed, illustrating the more popular models from the 1940s to the present time.

I must thank all the members of the American Truck Historical Society for offering their invaluable assistance in the making of this book.

A late 1940s Kenworth, owned by the late Joe Cash, where author spent most of his formative years observing and learning about trucks.

Last, but certainly not least, a special thanks to my wife, whose patience allowed for me to temporarily let normal home improvements take a "back seat" to this book.

Thanks: Autocar: Dennis Manchester, Greensboro, NC. Brockway: Colin Chisholm, Mack Truck Museum, Macungie, PA. Diamond T: American Truck Historical Society, Birmingham, AL; Joe Whitman, The New Diamond T Company, Lebanon, PA. Dodge Trucks: Don Bunn, Bloomington, MN; Tony Youngblood, (Dodge Bighorns), Augusta, GA. Ford Trucks: Bill Kellerman, Louisville, KY; George Schroyer, Celina, OH. Freightliner: American Truck Historical Society, Birmingham, AL. GMC Trucks: Dennis Manchester, Greensboro, NC; Mark Bridgwater, Claremont, CA; Thomas C. VanDegrift, Birmingham, MI. Hayes Trucks: Colin Chisholm, Mack Truck Museum, Macungie, PA.

International/Navistar: "Howdy" Hammill, Solon, IA; Gary Johnson, Wyanet, IL; Jerome Kubiniec, N. Tonawanda, NY; Bill Mortimer/Boerner Truck Center, Huntington Park, CA; Craig Smith, Campo, CA. Kenworth Trucks: Allen Koenig, Rochester, MN. Mack Trucks: Colin Chisholm, Mack Truck Museum, Macungie, PA. Marmon Trucks: John Scolastico, Jr., Marmon Motors, Garland, TX. Peterbilt Trucks: Hank Hamilton, Los Angeles, CA. Sterling Trucks: Fred J. Perkins, Weston, MA. Western Star Trucks: Don Hanson, Western Star Trucks, Kelowna, BC. White Trucks: Dennis Manchester, Greensboro, NC; Thomas Nobbe, Proconsul Public Relations, Cleveland, OH.

Special Thanks: Jerry Brody, Los Angeles, CA; Joe Cash (deceased), Fresno, CA; Jim Rowe, Twin Falls, ID.

Introduction
The Way it Was

Trucking today is a far cry from the days when a trucker didn't need a CB, when diesel fuel was under twenty cents a gallon, and when drivers stopped to help each other, regardless of who they were or who they drove for.

In earlier times, trucks were a bit primitive and took a lot of skill to operate. Horsepower was low and then there were the "two sticks," with which to shift.

Trucks were made of steel and so were the drivers. Truckers were generally clean-shaven, had short hair, wore pleated Frisco jeans and had either Pendleton shirts or a complete uniform (with hat) if they drove for a larger common carrier.

Today's trucks are a state of the art, with lighter components and more horsepower. The trucker of today is often referred to as "The Last American Cowboy." In times past, truckers were truckers and not cowboys. Bring back the past, when truckers would help each other . . . no drugs, no profanity, no CB, no "Lot Lizards." Just plain truckers with not a whole lot of fanfare.

Chapter 1

American Coleman

Ahead of its Time

Most folks, truckers included, have never heard of an American Coleman truck but the company, based in Littleton, Colorado, has been making truck components for many years. Since the 1930s, American Coleman has been a recognized leader in the production of snow-plowing equipment, axles, and transfer cases for the military, state governments, and other truck manufacturers.

Featured in these two pictures is American Coleman's interpretation of what a Class 8 big rig should be. Built in the late 1960s, this one-of-a-kind truck was officially called the Space Star. Unofficially, it was known by all as "the Batmobile" because of its aerodynamic design. Operating from Colorado, this unit delivered American Coleman products to various distributors in the eastern half of the United States.

The Space Star was all steel in construction and weighed in at 18,000lb. It had an 8V71N Detroit Diesel for power, an Eaton two-speed axle, and a Fuller transmission. It also had a

Overall view showing the Space Star, or "Batmobile" completely hooked up and ready to go.

Coleman chaindrive and a power-dividing transfer case, which had its own differential.

In addition to its styling, another thing that set the Space Star apart was the fact that it had no fifth wheel with which to connect the truck to the trailer. Instead, the truck's frame simply slid under its Comet Trailer and was locked into position by eight pins. This now made the trailer and tractor one unit.

Another interesting feature is the fact that the four single tires (no duals on this rig) could each steer simply by flipping a switch, thus affording better maneuverability. Fuel economy was excellent. The truck delivered 6.5mpg under all conditions, and this was almost thirty years ago.

If all that is not enough, this cab-over had two sleepers. One was located just above the driver, and the other was behind the driver. Also, the mufflers and exhaust stacks were located in the cab in their own closets, thus making for a quiet environment.

This photo illustrates just how high the Space Star sits, and how it is about to slide under the first trailer to become one unit. Overall length was 65ft, which was the legal length for that period of time.

The front bumper was made of T-100 high-tensile steel that could withstand almost any major impact. Can that be said of today's plastic components? Above the functional bumper, sat the 318hp engine on its own independent frame. Servicing the engine was simple: just roll the engine out, much the same way a drawer rolls out of a desk.

The Space Star only ran for a few years and it is not known why this rig disappeared. Perhaps for the same reason that the Tucker automobile disappeared . . . it was ahead of its time.

Chapter 2

Autocar

A Tradition of Strength

Autocar is one of the oldest names in the field of truck manufacturing. The company was founded in 1897 by Louis S. Clarke and his brother, John S. Clarke, and originally called The Pittsburgh Motor Vehicle Company. This name was to remain for two more years, until 1899, when the name was changed to Autocar. On January 1, 1900, the first shovel turned the first sod at Ardmore, Pennsylvania, to become the birthplace of what was to be one of America's most popular big rigs. A couple of other firsts: Autocar built the first universal shaft-driven models in the U.S., and pioneered the use of the first insulated porcelain spark plugs.

In 1908, in order to increase payload space, Autocar produced what was to be the first cab-over-engine designed truck. Autocar preferred to call it engine-under-seat design.

Ray Gookins' 1925 Autocar, named Old Betsy, is seen here in a 1968 photo. Power was supplied by a 390ci Ford V-8, backed by an Allison seven-speed automatic transmission. For over forty years, Ray and Old Betsy hauled for the Griffith Company of Los Angeles, building highways and bridges.

During the 1920s, Autocar built the popular gasoline-powered trucks and, as an alternative to gasoline power, also produced units with electric motors.

Most of the vehicles built during this time were designed as buses or to carry light freight. Autocar soon saw the need to enter the heavy transport sector of trucking, and began production of the Model 26. This truck boasted a six-cylinder engine and had three axles, thus enabling the company to be more competitive.

During the 1930s, Autocar expanded its line of trucks to include both conventional (engine/hood in front of cab), and further developed its cab-over config-uration. Autocar was also making inroads into such specialty vehicles as fire engine apparatus.

Like most of the truck and auto makers in the 1940s, Autocar was making vehicles for the

1941 U Model Autocar had integral sleeper cab, and exhaust stack on driver's side. Notice the "suicide" doors, common to all of the U Models. Power came via Detroit, Diesel, 238hp in-line six. This unit ran from Centralia, Illinois, to the West Coast as late as 1967.

military from the early 1940s until the end of the war in 1945.

In the mid-1940s, Autocar began reaching for Class 8 status and became a popular truck both to own as well as to drive. In all parts of the U.S., the name Autocar meant quality, as well as a good looking rig to have.

Class 8 status is the term given for the larger commercial vehicles that generally have three axles and are set up either as straight trucks or bobtails (the body on the frame of the vehicle), or as a three-axle tractor (the power

part of a tractor-trailer known as a semi). A class 8 rig can also be a two-axle tractor designed to pull either a longer semi trailer or a set of "doubles" (two trailers). For all intents and purposes, a Class 8 rig is the largest of the big rigs. Also, Class 8 rigs weigh more than 33,000lb gvw.

In 1953, Autocar was taken over by the White Motor Company of Cleveland, Ohio. Autocar was to keep its nameplate and became the producer of White's heaviest trucks, which were usually diesel-powered. The marque was given a separate identity by introducing a new

A 1983 Autocar Model AT64 is seen here, owned by Coy Youngblood of Pomona, California. Power is provided by a 3406 Caterpillar engine and backed by a thirteen-speed transmission. The AT64 Model was one of the most popular models ever produced by Autocar.

A 1988 Autocar is seen here at a construction operator's show. This is how the current Autocar appears. It has the look of Volvo-White-GM and is designed for construction, special applications, and off-highway use.

grille, which was fitted to all Autocars, and survives today on the White-GMC-Autocar trucks currently being produced. In 1974, production of the Autocar was moved from Pennsylvania to a newer plant in Ogden, Utah.

Also in the 1970s, Autocar began building a model called Construcktor. It was aimed at the construction industry, but never really caught on as a popular truck and was discontinued in 1985.

On the other side of the coin, the Autocar AT64 was the most popular rig traveling the Interstates and backroads, particularly in the West, and was being built into the mid-1980s.

On the last day of August 1981, the newly-formed Volvo-White Truck Corporation took over the products formerly marketed by the White Motor Corporation. This was to become a new era for White and Autocar trucks.

The New Family, as it was called, was now

Autocar conventional circa 1947. This low-mount was powered with a Cummins 150hp engine, backed with a five-speed main and three-speed auxiliary transmission.

Kings County Truck Lines ran this rig in the Los Angeles area, hauling milk.

making Class 8 trucks under the Volvo, White, and Autocar names and soon increased its share of the heavy truck sales from a low of 4.9% to over 10% of Class 8 truck sales in 1986.

Not long after this, GM was added to the nameplate, thus lending more credibility and the strength of one of America's most gigantic corporations.

Currently, the Autocar name is synonymous with off-highway hauling applications and in the field of construction. Current cab configuration was designed in the late 1980s, and resembles that of the Volvo-White.

While the AT64 has been discontinued, many are still seen in service, which is a tribute to Autocar's popular over-the-highway models of previous generations.

Chapter 3

Brockway

One Husky Truck

William N. Brockway started the Brockway Carriage Factory in Homer, New York, back in 1851. In 1889, the founder's son, George A. Brockway, took over full control of both the factory and all related business.

In 1912, the Brockway Motor Truck Company was organized, and moved all operations a few miles away to Cortland, New York. All stockholders were members of the Brockway family.

By 1917, the Brockway name was well established and were soon making Class B military trucks for the First World War. Because of their reliability, Brockway quickly adapted their rigs for civilian use after the war.

Brockway was not only a popular truck here in America, especially along the east coast, but was a much sought after truck in sixty-five other countries.

In 1928 Brockway acquired the Indiana Truck Corporation of Marion, Indiana. The

A three-axle tractor, series 300 seen at a 1969 truck and equipment show in Des Moines, Iowa.

Indiana Truck was well respected with a record of reliability. Together, both Brockway and Indiana were to prosper until the Great Depression of 1932, and because of a floundering economy, the Indiana Truck was to be one of the Depression's many casualties. As a result, Indiana Truck Corporation was sold to the White Motor Company. Brockway came out of the Depression, bruised but very much alive and continued to make a sturdy product until the Second World War.

Because of Brockway's reputation as a solid truck, the Army Corps of Engineers ordered a six-ton 6x6 chassis to transport rubber pontoons and steel treadways used in the building of combat bridges. Brockway successfully met all of the military's demands, and their excellent record was a boon to civilian sales at the war's end.

By 1946, Brockway was making heavy duty trucks known as the 260 series. The trucks were

This Brockway cab-over model was seen at the same Iowa equipment show. It is quite obvious that it was part of the Mack Truck Family, as it closely resembles the famous F Model Mack cab-over from the 1960s.

made of heavy gauge steel with some wood in the cabs–these rigs were built to last. 1956 saw Brockway become part of the Mack Truck dynasty, and two years later the famous "Huskie" line of Brockway trucks debuted.

In the style of its parent company's Bull-dog motto and logo, Brockway employed the Huskie to adorn the front of its trucks. 1962 was Brockway's Golden Anniversary, and the famous chrome Huskie gave way to a new gold-plated animal.

In 1963, Brockway built its first cab-over model, and in the mid-1960s brought out the 300 series. On this new series, swing-out front fenders became available, making the engine more accessible for drivers and mechanics. This popular innovation was also used by Dodge Trucks.

By 1976, Brockway had nine factory-owned branch sales and service facilities, and ninety-one independent dealers, primarily in the eastern United States.

During the first part of 1977, after an unauthorized strike by the local union, the production of Brockway trucks came to an abrupt halt. An additional forty-five trucks were built for Inter-American Transport of Miami, Florida. These trucks were for export to Iran, to be used in transporting sugar cane from the fields to the mills. The last Brockway to roll off the assembly line, serial number 91863, was on June 8, 1977, at one o'clock.

It is interesting to note, many of the Brockways built in the 1960s and 1970s found a new home in Puerto Rico, and are a fairly common truck there.

Once owned by Mattie Jordan, this rig, a 1946 Model 260, was originally one of many bobtail or straight trucks, run by the City Of Los Angeles, Dept. Of Water & Power. It was a three-axle unit and was later made into a two-axle and totally restored by The White Motor Company of Los Angeles. The tractor sports a Continental gasoline engine and this rig now has a home at the Mack Truck Museum.

Chapter 4

Diamond T

The Nation's Freight Car

Charles A. Tilt, the founder of Diamond T, took the name from his father's business, the Diamond Brand Shoe Company based in Chicago, Illinois.

In 1905, Tilt built his first motor cars on the north side of Chicago, and the Diamond T Motor Company was born. Production of various automobiles continued until 1910, when a Diamond T owner asked Tilt to build a truck to carry plumbing supplies. Taking on this new challenge, Tilt agreed, and thus Diamond T began its long venture into producing trucks. During its formative years, Diamond T was a regional rig, making trucks only for people in the Chicago area. However, due to its success, dealerships were soon popping up from coast to coast. In 1916, the company bought thirteen acres on Chicago's southwest side, and a 250,000sq ft plant, boasting of a 1,000ft assembly line was the "last word" in truck production for that time.

This 1950 Diamond T Model 910R is owned by Lee & Charmaine Hetterly of Everson, Washington. A Cummins 220hp engine lies under the hood.

The plant was in full swing when World War I had started, and Diamond T had built 1,500 Series B 3-to-5 ton Liberty trucks, with an additional 2,000 on order when the Armistice was signed.

By the late 1920s, Diamond T trucks had undergone a transformation and had a newer styling and completely new image. Having eighty distributorships in sixty foreign countries, a four-ton Diamond T was selling for just under $2000–a lot of money during the Great Depression.

In 1934 Diamond T built a modern, streamlined truck for Texaco. It was an airport refueling rig that carried 1,500 gallons of aviation fuel, was 26ft long, 92in wide, and 79in tall. The engine was located in the rear of the truck. A microphone was installed in the engine compartment which was connected to the cab, so that the driver could be told when to shift gears. This truck was so different that

A rare Reo cab-over, circa 1957. Reo built Class 8 trucks, but most of their models were much smaller. This rig was built before the nameplate changed to Diamond Reo.

it was featured at the Chicago World's Fair that year.

By 1936 Diamond T made more dramatic changes in styling and by 1937 had come out with its new COE (cab-over-engine), comparing it to the Burlington Zephyr, one of the beauti-

ful streamlined trains of the day. Among its many features was a slide-out engine for easy maintenance.

By 1940 the country was recovering from the Depression and Diamond T was alive and well. It was during this year that the company

This picture was taken on 26 April 1965 in Pomona, California, depicting an early 1960s Diamond T cab-over rolling over a set of portable scales manned by the California Highway Patrol. It was not known if the truck was overloaded.

startled the industry by offering a warranty covering their trucks for one year or 100,000 miles, whichever came first.

With the onset of World War II, Diamond T was making four-ton 6x6 trucks as well as half-tracks, and forty-five-ton tank transporters. Considered to be one of the best looking rigs in the Army, the transporter sported a 185hp Hercules diesel engine, with a four-speed main and three-speed auxiliary transmission, and could pull, fully loaded, at close to 25 mph. Building military equipment was, perhaps, Diamond T's most successful years.

After the war, Diamond T developed a station wagon–this was to be their "Edsel," and the idea was soon abandoned.

In 1950, in a joint venture with International Harvester, the two developed what was

Lollie Estrada leased this Diamond T cab-over, circa 1956, to Hopper Truck Lines of Phoenix, Arizona. Hopper was a popular trucking company which ran the southwest, hauling freight and cattle.

Several Diamond Ts can be seen here at a recent show put on by the American Truck Historical Society in Portland, Oregon.

to be known as the "comfort cab." Among the features were quick detachable fenders; a hood that brought outside air into the engine compartment, resulting in better fuel economy; and the four-point "diamond" mounting of the cab, sheet metal, and radiator. At the Chicago Auto Show, the truck underwent severe twisting for several hours, showing no structural damage to

any part of the rig. The introduction of the Model 950-951 also made its appearance in 1950, and was to be the largest Diamond T built at the Chicago facility. The 950 was brought out for western truckers, wanting more power and a larger radiator area for greater cooling. The first 950s had large gasoline engines, but it soon became apparent that diesel engines would be a better match for this highway heavyweight. The Tilt Cab (no pun intended) became available in 1953, and was later used by International Harvester.

In 1946, the company's founder, Charles Tilt, retired and in 1956, he died. By the late 1950s, Diamond T was in trouble. Reo was in a similar situation. Both companies were in competition with corporate giants International, GM, Ford, and White. In 1958, White Motor Company seized the opportunity to buy both Diamond T and Reo, and both operations were consolidated in Reo's Lansing, Michigan, plant in 1960. However, the new division, called Diamond Reo, continued to battle the tough economics and was sold to a southern investor who later sold it to Osterlund Incorporated of Harrisburg, Pennsylvania.

1967 was the last year Diamond Ts were built under that nameplate, and then it became Diamond Reo. The Diamond Reo continued up into the 1980s. In 1993 Osterlund sold out and that same year saw the birth of the New Diamond T Company.

Here is one of United's famous "Dirty Thirty," which were the top thirty elite owner-operators working for United Van Lines. This 1967 Diamond T was one of the last produced at the Lansing, Michigan, plant. The tractor originally sold for $30,100; power came via Cummins 335hp engine. This rig was owned by John Wilhelmsen of Rome, New York.

Chapter 5

Dodge Trucks
The Dependable Truck

The Dodge Truck history is really a conglomeration of several joint ventures. In the late 1800s, two brothers, Horace and John Dodge, got their start making bicycles in the Detroit area.

They were soon making parts for Ransom Olds (of Oldsmobile fame), and by 1901 were supplying the transmissions for the early Oldsmobile vehicles. Later, the brothers supplied parts for various Ford products.

It soon became apparent to the Dodge brothers that the demand for their products far exceeded their expectations, and began building cars under their own nameplate.

Buyers of Dodge automobiles soon talked the brothers into making a commercial vehicle, and by World War I, the Dodge Brothers emblem was a common sight on trucks. At the start of World War I, Dodge was there, making commercial chassis for the military. Other companies supplied bodies to suit the needs of the military. The Dodge commercial chassis was so successful that the U.S. government bought almost 20,000 Dodge vehicles in one form or another. John and Horace Dodge both died in 1920, never to see just how much their name was to figure in the molding of American transportation.

Around 1901, when the Dodge brothers were making parts for Olds, the Maxwell Motor Company, also from the Detroit area, was building cars with some degree of success. In 1917, Maxwell came out with its first truck, a one-ton rig powered by a four-cylinder engine. But by 1921, Maxwell had fallen on hard times. The Maxwell Motor Company was bought out by Walter Chrysler, who was determined to build a car bearing his own name. In 1925, he changed the name to Chrysler Corporation.

By 1928, Chrysler had also purchased Dodge Brothers. However, the story doesn't end there. In order to fill in the early history of Dodge, it is necessary to travel back in time to the early 1900s. Three brothers, Joseph, Robert, and Ray Graham, were in the glassblowing business in Indiana. They soon gave up this endeavor and turned their efforts to making chassis kits. Each kit would change an auto chassis into a commercial chassis, making it suitable for light-and medium-duty trucks.

In 1921 Graham Brothers entered into a joint-venture with Dodge. Graham used the Dodge chassis and Dodge marketed the Graham Trucks through their vast dealer network. The popularity of the Graham Brothers trucks was instantaneous, and they were soon were building buses as well as trucks, using Dodge engines for all of the power.

Dennis Hensiek of Carrollton, Missouri, owns this 1975 Dodge Bighorn, which he uses to haul grain for his farm. It is set up as a straight truck, or bobtail. This truck is an extremely rare breed, as Dodge built a total of only 261 of these vehicles, from 1973 to 1975.

By 1927 Dodge had purchased Graham Brothers, and was building trucks under the Dodge name only.

The next year, Walter Chrysler bought Dodge Brothers and thus Dodge became a part of the Chrysler Corporation we know today.

In the early 1930s, known as the Glamour Era for Dodge trucks, sales jumped dramatically. In 1933, sales jumped 362% over the previous year, due primarily to the new streamlined look of their trucks. The first Dodge Ram hood ornament appeared in the 1930s.

In 1937, safety was becoming a factor in truck manufacturing and Dodge was in the fore-front. The driver's environment was made safer by setting all dash controls flush, and thus free from any protruding panel switches or controls.

During the 1940s Chrysler launched the "Job-Rated" era. This is perhaps the most popular chapter in the Dodge Truck history, as the company started making inroads into larger commercial vehicles.

The late 1940s and early 1950s Dodge trucks are said to be from the "Pilot House" era and many of these vehicles are still in use.

Styling, safety, and mechanical improvements continued for Dodge and in February of 1964, the L series was born. This was a Class 8

rig with a Cummins diesel engine and was as big as any highway product built by Paccar or any other competitor. The L series was a cab-over model and was available as both a sleeper and as a non-sleeper. The L series was produced until 1975, at which time Dodge decided to discontinue its Class 8 cab-overs. The L series was a popular and rugged truck and was a favorite for long-distance use.

Around 1970, Dodge began the development of the Bighorn, a stately looking rig, capable of holding its own with any other Class 8 big rig. In 1971, approximately thirty Bighorns with butterfly hoods were built and delivered to a car-carrier. However, official production of this model began at the end of 1972, and a total of 261 Bighorns were built from 1973 to 1975. In 1975, Dodge decided to call it quits in the larger commercial vehicle department and once again confine its attention to successfully producing smaller vehicles and marketing its famous Ram pickup truck.

Of the 261 Bighorn Dodges produced, only about fifty can be found today, thus making them a much sought after truck to collect and restore.

It is pure speculation, however, but if the present Ram pickup was made available as a Class 8 vehicle, would there be enough support to make this the contemporary Bighorn?

Len McPherson leased this 1966 model LN1000 to Global Van Lines. The "L" meant that this was a tilt-cab model, and the "N" denotes diesel power. Dodge began producing the L1000 series in February 1964 and continued up to 1975 when all Class 8 production ceased.

Chapter 6

Ford Trucks

A Better Idea

Henry Ford and the Ford Motor Company are as much a part of American history as is the founding of America itself. Many books have been written about the man as well as his products, and this chapter will highlight some of Ford's developments in the truck division of the Ford Motor Company.

Ford produced its first official commercial vehicle in July of 1917, the one-ton Model TT. During the early years of Ford's truck division, the company boasted of the first light weight chassis, the first worm-drive rear axle, and the first use of solid rubber tires.

In 1924 Ford was no longer building just commercial chassis, but complete trucks. By 1928, Ford was fast becoming the truck to use in local hauling. The Model T soon gave way to the famous Model A. Ford was busy producing pickup trucks, delivery cars, ambulances, station wagons, police vehicles, and smaller Model A buses.

An early 1960s Ford conventional Model NTD with sleeper box. Although not exactly a popular model, Ford was definitely serious about capturing the Class 8 truck market.

With the onset of the Great Depression, many truck manufacturers fell on hard times and "bit the dust," which was not to be the case with Ford. As a matter of fact, while much of the competition was just trying to survive, Ford research and development department came out with many innovations that we take for granted, including dual rear wheels. The flat-head V-8 was found in the larger Ford rigs, as 1934 saw the final four-cylinder engines in Ford trucks.

By 1938 Ford's one-tonner became known as the model 350, and in 1939 Ford's 3/4-ton unit became known as the model 250. Ford trucks were so popular that they were the most common truck in both the larger cities and on the farms. Many of these older models are still in use today.

During World War II, Ford was in the front lines, supplying the military with vehicles such as personnel-carriers, Jeeps, and combat rigs like the half-tracks.

A beautiful example of the "Two-Story Falcon" of 1965. Seen here is Buck Harper's rig, leased to Warner Transfer of Ohio, agents for North American Van Lines.

After the war, Ford began gearing up for a larger share of the commercial market and in 1946 introduced their two-ton truck, and in 1948, Ford came out with the F series trucks. The series ranged from the F-1 to the larger F-8 series and the weight ranged from 2 1/2-ton trucks to the larger three-ton vehicles, which were powered by the mighty V-8 Lincoln engine. Also, air brakes became a standard feature on the larger Ford trucks.

During the 1950s, Ford was building its share of three-axle vehicles, and by the late

The W Model replaced the H Model, or "Two-Story Falcon." Seen here is a W Model, circa 1970.

1950s, more and more Fords were being used by the coast to coast van lines. These trucks were still, for the most part, gasoline-powered.

By the early 1960s, Ford became serious about capturing the lucrative Class 8 truck market and brought out the NTD model. This was a conventional that was durable as well as good-looking, retaining the lines of the Ford autos and smaller trucks of that era.

At about the same time, the H Model, or "Two-Story Falcon," made its debut. This was a stately vehicle that won the hearts of many an over-the-road driver. It was produced up until 1966.

The LTL Model Ford, this example with a fair amount of chrome. The LTL can hold its own to any Paccar product of similar size. This truck is pulling for United Van Lines of Missouri.

In 1966, the successor to the H Model came out in the form of the W Model cab-over. This particular model was more functional than beautiful; with the proper amount of chrome additions, the W Model found its place in the Class 8 market. This cab-over was produced until 1978, when it gave way to the CL model. During this time, Ford had great success marketing the L series conventional trucks, and its LTL was a popular rig for many small fleets and owner-operators. Also, it was as sharp-looking as anything Pacific Car & Foundry (Paccar), the parent company of both Kenworth and Peterbilt, was building.

The CL cab-over was produced until May of 1991 at the Ford Truck facility in Louisville, Kentucky, where most of the other large model commercial vehicles are built.

From the late 1980s until present, Ford's AeroMax is the truck of choice for many of the larger fleets as well as many of the small owner-operators. The AeroMax combines the toughness that Ford is famous for, plus the aerodynamics needed for today's fuel efficiency. Ford has "paid its dues." It is a well respected truck today and will be here tomorrow.

This CL Model was seen at a Las Vegas, Nevada, truck show. The CL was a favorite among truckers and was built until 1991 when production was phased out.

Bob Harris drives and maintains the pride of the Vons Grocery fleet, a 1989 AeroMax Ford. Harris runs this rig throughout Southern California delivering groceries to the many Vons stores.

Chapter 7

Freightliner
Custom Built Trucks

The Freightliner story is really about the marriage of two companies working together to build the perfect truck. Leland James was working for Consolidated Freightways in the 1930s. He never wanted to build trucks, but saw the need for making the heavier over-the-road trucks lighter, so that the payloads could be increased. He thought this could be easily accomplished by using more aluminum to build a lighter truck, thus increasing the truck's payload.

Consolidated Freight Lines (CF) started out in 1929, and their mechanics were always finding ways to lower operating costs by scavenging parts of other trucks and experimenting with other parts in order to improve downtime and lighten vehicle weight. The use of aluminum brake shoes and suspension hanger brackets was so successful that by 1936, entire truck and trailer bodies were being fabricated in Consolidated's shops.

Although not the most popular model produced by Freightliner, this rig is seen at the International Truck Show in 1992 celebrating Freightliner's 50th Anniversary.

By the mid-1930s, the mechanics at Consolidated's Portland, Oregon, shops were tinkering with the cab-over-engine design. In 1937 a Fageol was reconstructed employing the cab-over style and a Cummins six-cylinder diesel engine was used to supply the power.

By 1940, Leland James and his Freightways partners founded Freightways Manufacturing Company, Inc. a Utah-based corporation. It was to be a joint venture, building light weight aluminum trucks for a group of trucking companies operating in the Western states.

The first "Freight-Liner" was hyphenated, appearing in 1940. It was during that same year that the first truck rolled out, based at CF's terminal in Billings, Montana. The first rig bearing the "Freightliner" nameplate was built the following year.

As World War II was developing in Europe, another smaller war had begun on the homefront. The U.S. Justice Department had charged

Restored by ten retired CF mechanics all in their sixties and seventies, this 1947 Freightliner truck and trailer took over 4,000 hours to completely restore.

Freightways, Inc. with having a monopoly in restraint of trade, and the federal government brought suit to dissolve the Freightways cooperative. As a result, the Freightways Manufacturing Company became the Freightliner Corporation. After a two year court battle, the carriers involved with Freightways agreed to end their affiliation with truck manufacturing. The Utah facility was moved to Portland, Oregon, to wait out WWII. After the war, Freightliner came back even stronger and more committed to using aluminum in every phase of making a sturdier and

Pictured under the concrete dinosaur at Cabazon, California, is a 1960, 72in sleeper cab Freightliner. This popular model is owned by Charles Olivieri of Bakersfield, California.

lighter Class 8 truck.

It was in 1947 that Freightliner came out with the Model 800, better known as the "Bubblenose" cab-over. Also that year, the truck became available for the general public, which meant that Freightliner's credibility was equal to that of its competition. In 1950 the Hyster Company of Portland became the first private carrier to buy a Freightliner with an integral sleeper, the Model 900, which was the first transcontinental tractor having this sleeper set up. This particular rig was restored in 1976 and is now on display at the Smithsonian Institution.

During the 1940s, Freightliner also built a

Freightliner is famous for building the unusual, and this cattle truck is no exception. Note the penthouse sleeper located above the driver–watch out for those low bridges!!

The "Destroyer" is the Freightliner answer to Ford's "Big Foot." Based out of Ellensburg, Washington, the Destroyer is a 1969 model, guaranteed to be a crowd-pleaser at any truck show.

conventional truck, the Model 600, but it was the much more popular "Bubblenose" that was aggressively marketed. From this time to the present, Freightliner has been known for custom-building trucks, and their "can do" policy of building the unusual continues today.

In 1951 Freightliner signed an exclusive sales and service agreement with the White Motor Company, and this explains why the name White Freightliner appeared on so many nameplates. Over 100,000 White Freightliners were sold through the various White dealerships in the U.S. and Canada.

In 1958, Freightliner claimed the first tilt-

Kurt Smistik of Livermore, California, owns this sharp 1981 conventional. A 400hp Cummins engine keeps "Garfield the Cat" running.

cab cab-over, and two years later produced their Model WFT7242, having a 72in sleeper cab.

In the late 1960s, Freightliner produced its first big sleeper cab, a 107in unit going to trucker Ed Douthitt of Montana. Several years later, Paccar followed the Freightliner lead, making a 110in sleeper cab-over.

In 1981, Daimler-Benz bought Freightliner and sales of this truck continued to grow, and in 1992 they controlled a 23.2 percent share of the Class 8 truck market. Large carriers such as Werner Enterprises, C.R. England, Swift Transportation, and of course Consolidated Freightways are but a few of the companies that know the advantages of owning Freightliner.

Given Freightliner's popularity, aggressive sales and dependable service policy, they have earned a place in trucking's Haul Of Fame . . . and to think it all started in a garage by a guy who pioneered the use of a new metal, aluminum.

Rebel Oil Co. of Las Vegas, Nevada, can "legal" over 13,000 gallons of gasoline on this twin-steering Freightliner truck and trailer super tanker. Note single tires on the trailer.

Chapter 8

GMC
A Success Story

Who would have thought that two brothers named Max and Morris Grabowsky, along with two saloonkeepers, Barney Finn and Albert Marx, were to be the pioneering founders of what is known today as the General Motors Corporation.

Starting in the Detroit area in 1900, the Grabowsky brothers developed a commercial truck powered by a one-cylinder horizontal engine which was sold in 1902.

Business continued as normal until 1908 when William C. Durant came into the picture and the Grabowsky Motor Vehicle Company became the General Motors Company. In 1916 the General Motors Corporation was born.

That same year, 1916, saw the first husband/wife team make the first transcontinental trip in a truck. Driving a Model 31 GMC, Mr. and Mrs. William Warwick drove from Seattle,

Pete Dykstra of Ontario, California, owns this 1952 900 series GMC. A 671 Detroit Diesel and a five and three transmission gets this rig down the highway.

Washington, to New York City in a little over two months, covering over 3,640 miles.

As part of the World War I effort, GM supplied more than 8,000 trucks with various body types to the Army from 1917 to 1919. Shortly after the war, GM began improving assembly line techniques at its Pontiac, Michigan, plant and started "piggybacking" their vehicles onto railroad cars to their various destinations.

1925 was a momentous year, as The Yellow Cab Manufacturing Company of Chicago, with roots going back to 1908, became part of GMC. GMC now had the flexibility to make both smaller and larger trucks with the GMC nameplate.

During the 1920s, the country was dealing with the 18th amendment, which prohibited the manufacture or consumption of alcoholic beverages. However, bootleggers to the north in

Mark Bridgwater of Claremont, California, owns this 1954 model series 630 "Jimmy." It sports a 471 engine and a five and three transmission. Notice the one-piece windshield.

Canada were alive and well, supplying alcohol to a thirsty United States and their choice of truck was GMC. As a matter of fact, by the end of the twenties, GMC was one of the most popular trucks in both the public and private sectors.

The T series was born in 1927, and by 1931 the T-95 was one of the first of the Class 8 trucks. It sported a three-axle configuration, air brakes, four-speed transmission, and could carry payloads up to fifteen-tons.

GM was not immune to the Great Depression, and in an effort to reduce operating costs, expenses and personnel were cut to a minimum.

Next page
Mike Ottonello owned and restored this 1948 A Model long hood conventional. This rig was originally owned by Parker Truck Co. of San Diego, California. The trailer was supplied by Coast Distribution of San Diego.

41

A comparison picture shows the bubblenose GMC cab-over of the 1950s next to a "Crackerbox" cab-over of the 1960s, both pulling for Global Van Lines.

A late 1980s GMC General seen here set up as a bobtail, or straight truck. This truck is owned by Great Western Litho of Los Angeles.

At about this time, GM came out with a new line of trailers. This line-up included semis, four-wheelers and six-wheelers. Almost 400 of these units were built before the end of 1931, and production of these trailers continued throughout the 1930s.

In 1934 GMC built its first cab-over model which was delivered to Bekins Van and Storage. By 1937, a new streamlined design graced that year's new trucks and wider choice of colors became available. By 1939 GMC had introduced its "A" model rigs, with AC, ADC, AF, and ADF models numbered 100 to 850 inclusive.

When America went to war in 1941, GMC once again stood ready to supply the military with new vehicles and innovations. One of these was the Model DUKW Amphibian vehicle

A group of new 1969 Astro 95s lined up for a sales promotion at Hollywood Park in Inglewood, California.

which could travel on land as well as on water, carrying troops and equipment. Obviously, this vehicle would be known as the "Duck," and came in three handy sizes: two-four-and eight-ton.

In the mid-to late 1940s, GM enjoyed great popularity and sales were consistent even though there were no significant style changes.

In March of 1949, the A Model was phased out and gave way to a whole new body style for the Class 8 truck. At the year's end, the H Model was born and was to remain throughout the 1950s as GM's only Class 8 truck. A "Bubblenose" cab-over also became available, and a factory sleeper was available as an option. The 900s were the larger Class 8 vehicles, with lower numbers denoting smaller vehicles.

The last of the "Bubblenose" cab-overs came out in 1959, and were replaced by what was to be known as the "Crackerbox" series, so named because it had such a square look. Both sleeper and nonsleeper models were built, and this rather stately-looking unit was produced from 1959 until 1968.

In 1968, a new cab-over truck was unveiled by the folks at GM. The Astro 95 was born and became an instant success. It had an

all new wrap-around dashboard, an improved windshield area for better visibility and a completely redesigned cab. It was offered as either a sleeper or a nonsleeper.

During the evolution of the Astro, the windshield became even larger, as did the radiator area in order to improve the cooling of larger diesel engines. 1987 saw the end of Astro production. Not to be overlooked, the massive H Model conventional of the 1950s gave way to the 9500 series in 1966. It, too, was an impressive rig with its long fiberglass hood. When pulled forward, there was plenty of room to house any diesel engine, including the V-12 Detroit Diesel (part of the GM family).

On January 1988, GMC became part of the Volvo-White group of truck manufacturers and is going strong today, building trucks under the "New Family," incorporating Volvo-White-GMC and Autocar.

Though the GMC nameplate may be gone from the newer Class 8 trucks of today, many of the older models are still in use. The Grabowsky brothers, Barney Finn and Albert Marx would be proud of their joint-venture.

Here is a Brigadier with its hood pulled forward, showing an 8V71 Detroit Diesel engine, also from the Hollywood Park show.

Chapter 9

Hayes Trucks
Built To Last

"Built To Last," was more than a motto for this Canadian-built truck.

The company's roots date back to 1920, when W.E. Anderson and Douglas Hayes of Vancouver, British Columbia, formed the Hayes-Anderson Motor Co. Ltd. The first two years saw the two men marketing U.S.-built trucks for the rough terrain of western Canada. However, the American trucks were simply not strong enough for the heavy payloads of the logging industry, so they started building their own logging trucks. In 1928 the name of Hayes-Anderson gave way to Hayes Mfg. Co. Ltd., although Hayes-Anderson appeared on trucks until 1934.

Not content with building only trucks, Hayes also made moving vans, dump trucks, tankers, tractors, buses, and trailers. The company made just about everything for loggers and truckers except engines and drivetrains, which were to be supplied by other vendors.

This photo shows a 1960s Hayes Clipper cab-over model, seen here at Mike & Vic's Truck Stop south of Toledo, Ohio, in 1965.

By 1933, diesel engines were beginning to prove themselves and Hayes was the first manufacturer of logging trucks to offer diesel engines. Hayes was also the first to offer dual axles on their logging trucks, which increased payload capacity.

By 1935 log hauling had become a big business in British Columbia, and the company began to specialize in building the massive over-sized logging trucks and trailers. Logging trucks, as well as other huge off-highway products were the "bread and butter" for Hayes, and some of the largest custom built rigs ever built in Canada were from their Vancouver factory.

In 1946, Hayes merged with Lawrence Manufacturing, producers of other logging equipment, and introduced the HDX series of off-highway logging trucks in 1949.

In addition to their success in the logging industry, Hayes' trucks are popular in the oil fields as well sugar plantations, where they haul

Seen here, on the island of Kauai, is a 1970s vintage Hayes, hauling for the Lihue Plantation. Lihue is a leading producer of sugar cane.

heavy loads off-highway. Hayes also tried its hand at building a truck for highway use with the introduction of the Clipper series. It was available as both a conventional and a cab-over and was used by truckers in both Canada and by operators in the lower forty-eight states.

In 1969 Mack Trucks bought into Hayes, and both companies continued to prosper. Truck production rose from fifty a year to 500,

not a bad jump in sales. However, in 1974 Mack found it necessary to sell Hayes. The Gearmatic Co. Ltd., a division of Paccar, took over and phased out the mighty Hayes truck in 1975.

Although no new Hayes trucks have been built since 1975, many are still in use, which brings us back to the Hayes motto: "Built To Last."

Chapter 10

International/Navistar

Going Strong

Over 150 years and still going strong–quite an accomplishment for any company, but for International Harvester Company (IH) it has been one tempered with both success and failure.

To fully comprehend the enormity of this corporate giant, it is necessary to trace its roots to 1831, when Cyrus Hall McCormick introduced his reaper, a crude farm implement. From this meager beginning came the IH which was formed in 1902.

Unlike any other truck manufacturer, IH produced a vast array of agricultural equipment, from manure spreaders to cotton pickers, long before the truck was thought of. International also found success with refrigerators, freezers, and air conditioners.

In order to appreciate of current Class 8 trucks produced by International, or Navistar as it is now called, a little company history is necessary.

An International "Cherrypicker" of the 1950s shown here as a truck and trailer with integral sleeper. P.I.E. had a fleet of these rigs, but lowered the cab 8in so that a Thermo King reefer unit would work better when mounted on the nose of the trailer.

Credit must be given to E.A. Johnston, who started designs for the International Auto-Buggy in 1905, and began production in 1907. By 1912 IH was a credible truck builder producing vehicles with both air-cooled and water-cooled engines. In 1915, five new models became available, ranging from 3/4-ton up to 3 1/2-ton, designated as models H, F, K, G, and L. All had four-cylinder engines and were produced until 1923. Standard equipment included artillery wheels with solid rubber tires. Pneumatic tires were optional on all models except for the larger 3 1/2 ton model, for which they were standard.

IH is one of the largest builders of medium (Class 7) diesel engines today, offering engines from 175 to 300hp.

In 1928, IH was building trucks with two-speed rear axles and was one of the first to offer this feature. Also during 1928, IH made a proto-

In the mid 1980s, Navistar came out with the 8300 series, which featured a newly designed cab. With its one-piece flat windshield and aerodynamic style, this rig has been also down-sized with smaller model numbers to meet the needs of Class 7 markets.

type diesel engine. 1934 saw IH completely revamp styling to make their square and functional-looking rigs more streamlined and aerodynamic.

By 1936 "Cornbinders," an IH nickname, were in full production of the large six-wheeled trucks. Between 1938 and 1940, the "D" series appeared, followed by the "K" series. The K series trucks were used extensively during World War II and remained quite popular after the war.

In 1946, IH began to seriously pursue the Class 8 truck market by up-scaling the K series. The larger three-axle was available with either a Continental gasoline engine or a Cummins diesel. Truck plants were located in Emeryville, California, and Fort Wayne, Indiana.

Also in 1946, IH introduced the "Westcoaster." It sported a cab large enough for three people and had two very large two-piece rectangular windshield. It was a massive-looking rig and came powered either by gas or diesel. A "W" model cab-over Westcoaster came out to complement the conventional. Both were produced from 1946 to 1949. The W series closely resembled the bullnose Kenworth cab-over of that era; its windshield was more square whereas the Kenworth's had rounded the corners.

1949 saw the last of the famous K series, with the KB model, the largest K series truck built for on-highway application. In 1950 IH, along with Diamond T, introduced the Comfo-Vision cab which was more driver-friendly and boasted of a slightly curved, one-piece windshield.

Many changes were taking place at IH in the early 1950s with the introduction of the "L" series and "R" series from 1953 to 1955.

During the 1950s, IH came out with the much sought-after RDF 405, which many of people incorrectly refer to as the Westcoaster. The only thing that the RDF 405 and the Westcoaster have in common is the same parking light lens, everything else is completely different.

Pictured here is a 1965 Emeryville, powered by a Cummins 335hp engine. The Emeryville enjoyed great popularity coast to coast but was phased out in 1965.

Jerry Noordman of Enumclaw, Washington, restored this 1959 conventional. Powered by a 220hp Cummins engine, this rig has a five-speed main and four-speed auxiliary transmission.

Next page
"Dickybird" Robinson drove this 1980 Transtar 4300 series and was known as "The Legend of Interstate 15." This rig turned heads from Las Vegas to Los Angeles.

Along with the long-hood Comfo-Cab conventional came the "Cherrypicker." It was a cab-over available either as a non-sleeper or with an integral sleeper and in the early 1950s was the truck of choice for Pacific Intermountain Express (P.I.E.), one of the nation's top freight companies. Later this model was to become known as the "R" series.

In the late 1950s, IH made yet another new cab-over called the "Emeryville," which was also known as the "Highbinder."

The Emeryville of the late 1950s had a two-piece windshield and came either as a sleeper or non-sleeper model. This particular truck enjoyed great success on both coasts, and was available up to 1965.

At approximately the same time that this newer styled Emeryville was in production, IH came out with an upgrade available only as a conventional model. This was the DC model and came with an integral sleeper though few were actually built. This truck achieved great success in various applications, especially in the construction field. These DC trucks were

The DC Model International came out in the early 1960s and became known as the "Donald Duck" International by western operators. This truck was a favorite truck in the construction industry; production continued into the 1970s.

referred to as "Donald Duck" Internationals. They featured a large two-piece windshield with a tilting fiberglass front end, and were produced into the early 1970s.

As the Emeryville was being phased out in 1965, another new cab-over was to make its debut in the form of the CO-4000. This rig was a departure from previous models and was to set the trend for future IH cab-overs. The CO-4000 was built from 1965 to 1967.

In 1968 the larger CO-4070A was phased in to allow for larger diesel engines to function more efficiently. By 1974 the CO-4070B was offered and was the first model to incorporate the name Transtar in its nameplate.

By 1981 the CO-9670 was replacing the Transtar of the 1970s. The newer 4300 conventional series was very a popular rig. This model was actually born in the 1970s, but was refined in the 1980s.

Around 1980, IH began to suffer from some very serious problems. A long strike from 1979 to 1980 hurt production, and the farm crisis of 1980 compounded matters, causing a big loss in farm sales. The federal government's mandate on cleaner, more efficient, and lighter engines brought International to its knees. On February 20, 1986, IH changed its name to Navistar, and sold its farm equipment division to Case-Tenneco, which insisted on retaining the International Harvester logo.

The divesting of the farm equipment division may have been a blessing in disguise, as Navistar is definitely on the comeback trail, making greater inroads in both Class 7 and Class 8 truck sales. Current production of Navistar conventional and construction trucks is ongoing at the Chatham, Ontario, plant in Canada and cab-overs and medium-sized trucks are being assembled in Ohio at the Springfield facility.

Though Navistar was on shaky ground for a while, it has proven that even under adverse conditions, this company is still going strong. International Harvester/Navistar has built more truck models than any other manufacturer and will continue to build trucks in the future.

The CO-4000 replaced the Emeryville in 1965 with an entirely new cab. This style was to remain for several years, becoming more refined as different models were added.

Chapter 11

Kenworth Trucks
King of the Road

The Kenworth of today is the result of years of evolution and is a far cry from its beginnings in 1915 as the Gerlinger Mfg. Co. of Portland, Oregon. In 1917, the Gerlinger name gave way to Gersix, and the company moved from Oregon to the Seattle, Washington, area. In 1923 the names of the two major stockholders, H.W. Kent and E.K. Worthington were combined to create the name "Kenworth."

The Kenworth (KW) truck was born out of the need to fulfill the demands of the timber and logging industry of the northwest, as well as for meeting the newer challenges set forth by agriculture and mining in other parts of the country.

In the early 1920s, it was not uncommon for Kenworth dealers to take in old "Dobbins" as a trade-in on a Kenworth truck. Perhaps this is where the term "horse-trading" got its start.

The 1930s shovelnose Kenworth seen here is owned by Van Dyke Dairy of Fallon, Nevada. Windwings did not become available until the late 1940s. Headlights on this rig appear to be a more modern version found on Peterbilt trucks.

During this period, two truck manufacturers, Vulcan and H.R.L., decided to close their doors and Kenworth bought all of their parts and patterns.

With the onset of the depression, Kenworth continued to grow as many of their competitors fell by the wayside. Kenworth was the first to offer factory installation of a six-cylinder gasoline engine.

In 1935 Kenworth began experimenting with aerodynamic design and was experimenting with the idea of the cab-over-engine design. The following year, the Model 516 was introduced as Kenworth's first on-highway COE, designed to meet Arizona's strict length law limit. At about the same time, KW was making inroads, refining their conventional truck, and the "shovelnose" appeared as part of the Kenworth line-up in the 1930s.

In the early 1990s, Kenworth reintroduced the long-hood with its W900L Model. Cliff Hiller of Union Beach, New Jersey, drives this long-hood for Cumberland Packing of Brooklyn, New York.

During World War II, Kenworth built military vehicles, the M-1 and M-1A1 wreckers, as well as creating nose assemblies for various aircraft. In 1944 Kenworth became a subsidiary of Pacific Car & Foundry (known as Paccar).

After the war, Kenworth continued to refine both the cab-over and the conventional model trucks, and in 1949 came out with "The Bruck." It was a combination bus and truck and though it was never widely accepted, it showed what quality engineering could do. Kenworth was no newcomer to designing and building

buses, and offered several models in the 1930s, as well as earning a well-respected name in the area of fire fighting apparatus.

In the early 1950s, both the cab-over and conventional models were quite popular with owner-operators and larger fleets. Engines changed from 150hp to the larger 220hp Cummins motor, and the five-speed main and three-speed auxiliary transmission were typical.

The mid-1950s was a time of change and upheaval in the trucking industry. Laws restricting length and weight changed and

A Kenworth conventional, circa 1948, is seen here at Stauffer Chemical Company. Post Transportation was the owner and ran mostly Kenworths in its fleet of chemical-hauling trucks. This style remained basically unchanged during the late 1940s and into the 1950s.

The popular Kenworth "Bull-Nose" of the 1950s is seen here in a truck and trailer application hauling livestock for Chanley Bros. Livestock Transportation of Bakersfield, California. When they were in business, Chanley ran the western states hauling livestock in various model KWs.

In 1954 Kenworth introduced the CBE (cab-beside-engine) model. It left something to be desired in the way of looks but filled the need of a lighter truck with better visibility.

Kenworth brought out this new cab-over in 1955, the Model 521 with a 72in sleeper cab. It is shown here unloading cattle in 1956 at the Los Angeles Union Stockyards in Vernon, California.

Next page
"Ol' Blue®" is a 1951 KW Model 525, and is perhaps the most famous Kenworth of them all. Ol' Blue® is owned by RJ Taylor, and has been featured in just about every trucking publication in the U.S., as well as in many foreign countries. Ol' Blue® is the centerpiece of The United Safety Alliance, Inc. dba Ol' Blue® USA This rig has a 400hp engine, an eighteen-speed transmission, Michelin tires, Alcoa aluminum wheels, and a Neway air-ride suspension on a 276in wheelbase. The sleeper was specially made by Mercury Fabricators in 1966 for this rig. Ol' Blue® has received the endorsement of state and local law enforcement agencies across the country, the support of Mothers Against Drunk Drivers (M.A.D.D.), the backing of the Los Angeles City Unified School District, and received federal funding in furthering highway safety. Ol' Blue® is a *working* truck, having hauled the Apollo 14 Spacecraft in 1973.

Kenworth was there to meet the new challenge.

In 1954 KW came out with the newly designed COE called the CBE (Cab-Beside-Engine) model. It was a half-cab that boasted increased visibility for the driver, and was lighter in weight, thus affording more payload. ICX, Denver-Chicago Trucking, and Garrett Freight Lines were but a few of the common carriers that purchased these rigs.

Shortly after the introduction of the CBE, Kenworth came out with the Model 521, a newly designed cab-over that was to replace the popular "Bullnose" that dominated the 1940s and 1950s. The Model 521 was built in con-junction with the Bullnose, which was finally phased out in the late 1950s.

In 1957 the short-lived Model 521 gave way to yet another style of cab-over, called the CSE (Cab-Surrounding-Engine). It was refined, made into a tilt-cab for easier engine accessibility. If you were to park a 1957 CSE next to today's cab-over model, you would see a striking similarity in the appearance of the two, especially in the windshield configuration.

At the beginning of 1959, Kenworth offered "Uniglas" for the conventional models. Uniglas offered an all-fiberglass front end that could be pulled forward ninety degrees to expose the engine for easier servicing. The Uniglas

The first wide-hood by Kenworth made its debut in 1962 as the Model 925. This is the author's favorite KW as it combined the traditional Kenworth cab of the 1940s through the 1950s with the wide hood found in trucks of today. Siefert Bros. Trucking of Du Quoin, Illinois, ran this truck from the midwest to the west coast hauling perishables.

"The Boss Truck Of America" is a 1970 Kenworth featuring a chrome V-12 Detroit Diesel engine under its long hood. The rig is owned by Jerry Malone of Tulare, California, and is featured at state fairs, shopping centers, car and truck shows, and similar events coast to coast.

front end did not replace the standard butterfly hood, but gave the operator an new option.

By 1961 Kenworth was making the S-900 series conventional. It was the forerunner to the famous "Ant-Eater" that was to become so popular years later.

About a year later, in 1962, Kenworth came out with their first wide-hood conventional, which is this author's favorite truck. The Model 925 combined the traditional look of the smaller Kenworth cab, windshield, and Uniglas

front end with a much larger radiator. Actually, it was 400in larger to accommodate the newer, larger engines. The Model 925 was built only for a few years. In 1964 KW came out with a newly designed conventional cab with a much larger windshield. This was to be one of the final years of the older style cab that had been around and refined since the 1940s.

During the mid-1960s, the butterfly hood gave way to the Uniglas front end, with the exceptions of the larger off-highway models

Ken Weiland's 1973 Model W900 is seen here taking on a load of lumber. Weiland is a true owner-operator who gets his own loads and leases to nobody. Weiland runs in California, Oregon, Nevada, and New Mexico hauling lumber, nursery products, steel, refrigerated commodities and general freight and is based in Sylmar, California.

Shown here is a small fleet of "Ant-Eaters" circa 1988. The Model T600 is a far cry from its ancestor of 1961, the S-900 series. By improved aerodynamics, the Ant-Eater boasts increased fuel mileage, and is perhaps Kenworth's most popular contemporary truck.

used in oil field, sugar cane, and logging applications. By the late 1960s, Kenworth offered the regular as well as the long-nosed hood for their conventionals. The longer hoods could accommodate the larger V-12 Detroit Diesel engines, among others.

Although the long-hood models were phased out in the early 1980s, a few were still being produced in smaller numbers up until 1984. Kenworth discontinued the longer hood models in the mid-1980s, but the demand was so great and the competition from Peterbilt was so strong that in the early 1990s, Kenworth brought back a long-hood model with the W900L and continues to market this unit with great success.

Remembering the S-900 series of 1961, the "Ant-Eater" of the 1980s brought the focus of

The Kenworth Aerodyne cab-over is seen here at a recent truck show. This truck is designed with the owner-operator in mind. If it was parked next to the KW cab-over tilt cab of the late 1950s, the similarities would be striking.

aerodynamics to the forefront of Class 8 truck design. The Ant-Eater has been refined and continues to be popular both in one-and two-piece windshield configurations. Kenworth, among others, sees the ever growing market in the smaller Class 7 size trucks and are down-sizing the more popular Class 8 models to fill this niche in trucking.

In addition to becoming the first to install a six-cylinder motor from the factory, other Kenworth "firsts," include: The FIRST gas turbine powered truck in scheduled freight service. This was in 1953 in a butterfly hood conven-

tional pulling for West Coast Fast Freight, running from Seattle to Los Angeles. The FIRST factory installed aluminum diesel engine in a motor truck, the FIRST extruded aluminum frame, the FIRST cab-beside-engine highway transport rig, the FIRST threaded springs pins and bushings in a truck, and the FIRST dual-drive torsion bar spring bogie.

Kenworth will continue to be a leader in manufacturing both on and off highway diesel trucks, as long as creative engineering and exhaustive testing, combined with rigid quality control and driver input continue to flourish.

Chapter 12

Mack Trucks

The Bulldog is Alive and Well

John and Augustus Mack experimented with trucks and buses in the late 1890s, and sold their first unit in late 1900, thus making Mack the oldest continuous truck builder in North America. Mack Brothers Wagon Works was the name for this early pioneer of truck and bus manufacturing, and the base of operations was in Brooklyn, New York.

In 1905 the young company was experiencing such growth that a move was made out of the Brooklyn area and a new factory established in Allentown, Pennsylvania, for both truck and bus production.

Mack is a respected builder of fire engines as well as trucks and buses, and in 1910 delivered the first motorized fire truck, a hook and ladder rig, to the City of Morristown, New Jersey. The following year saw Mack sell the first engine-driven fire pumper to the City of Cynwyd in Pennsylvania.

Warren Hetterly's 1957 B-61 is seen here. The B Model was one of the most popular Mack trucks ever built.

1916 was a significant year for Mack, as it introduced the famous AC Model and the Bulldog identity was born. A total of 40,299 ACs were built over the next twenty-three years and 4,470 of them saw action in World War I.

Shortly after the end of the war Mack initiated the use of both air cleaners and oil filters on truck engines to extend operating life, reduce maintenance, and provide a greater savings to customers.

In the late 1920s, Mack began experimenting with high speed diesel truck engines, and has since made some of the finest truck engines. Mack is one of the only truck producers to build its own engines, transmissions, and rear ends. Other manufacturers use outside sources to supply components making up the drivetrain.

In the 1930s, Mack was on the cutting edge of motor vehicle technology. In 1931 Mack was the first to employ power steering for

a bus. During the thirties, Mack was also the first to apply the use of four wheel brakes to heavy trucks. In 1938 Mack introduced the first diesel engine designed especially for trucks.

By 1940 Mack was making the now-famous L Model conventional truck, and this rig was to gain popularity on both the east and west coasts. Mack Trucks did its share during the World War II years, building over 35,000 vehicles for the military with 16,000 of those being powered by Mack diesel engines.

After the war, Mack returned to civilian production and in 1947 the LT Model was born. This model was considered by many to be "The Duesenberg Of Diesels," and were built in Allentown until 1956.

The 1950s was a decade of many changes for Mack Trucks, and a variety of models evolved, bringing forth new transmissions and rear ends.

This W series Mack, circa 1955 was owned by Allan Arthur. The trailers were set up to carry cattle, and molasses was carried in the compartments under both trailers. Allan Arthur was a livestock hauler operating in the western states.

1953 was a milestone year, as several new models were offered for the first time. The B series (B20 through B87) became a reality and was to continue until 1966, producing a total of 127,000 B Models and 47,459 Model B61s, one of the most popular trucks ever built by Mack.

In 1953, Mack also produced the W Model cab-over. This was the Bulldog's answer to the "Bullnose" Kenworth, and the "Bubblenose" cab-overs offered by Peterbilt and White Freightliner. The W Model received great acceptance by western operators, and was designed in both sleeper and non-sleeper models; production ended in 1958.

Finally, 1953 saw yet another new model make its debut, the legendary H Model, also known as the "Cherrypicker," because it stood so tall. It soon became a common sight along America's new Interstates. The "Cherrypicker" soon gave way and in 1956 the last one rolled out of the assembly plant. The mighty H60 and H61 were replaced by similar versions, the H62 and H63, which were built from 1954 to 1959. They bore a strong resemblance to the "Cherrypicker" but were lower in stature. From 1958 to 1962 the H67 was produced. It, too, resembled its cousin the H60 Model, but the H67 sported dual headlights. All previous models had had single headlights mounted separately from the front fenders.

Mack had been a leader in the design and fabrication of electric, diesel, and gasoline-powered buses, but 1960 saw the last complete bus produced.

With the phasing out of the H Model came phasing in of the G Model cab-over, which was equally successful. It was one of the first Class 8 trucks to offer easy entry by lowering the outside door handle to the bottom of the door. This model, like all Mack cab-overs, was available in both sleeper and non-sleeper models and was produced from 1959 to 1962.

In 1962 Mack unveiled its famous F Model cab-over. It was built on both the east coast and

Referred to by many as "The Duesenberg Of Diesels," this 1953 LT Mack is owned by Jake DeWitt of Tolleson, Arizona. LTs were produced from 1947 to 1956.

the west coast at a new plant in Hayward, California, to meet the demands of western truckers. The F Model was so popular that production continued until 1982, and many F Models can still be seen on today's highways.

By 1975 Mack had reintroduced two models of the W series, the WL and WS, which were built in both Allentown and Hayward. In 1980 all production of the WL and WS shifted to Allentown.

1982 saw the advent of a newer and more massive-looking cab-over called the MH. This rig was to be produced domestically up to January 1, 1994. The MH is still in production, but for export only.

Drawing on the popularity of the Bulldog conventional, Mack came out with the R Model in 1965. From 1965 to 1987, Mack produced over 210,000 of this model.

The RS and RL Models, much lighter versions of the R, came out in 1966. They were designed and built in Hayward to meet the needs of western operators as well the demands of the construction industry.

A 1974 F Model Mack owned by the Los Angeles City Fire Department is seen as a wrecker parked in front of Station 27, which is now a fire museum in Hollywood.

This comparison picture shows an MH Mack (on the left) beside an H67 owned by Race Horse Express of Wildomar, California.

Here is a Mack Super Liner (on the left) and its newer replacement, the CH Model owned by Robertson's Ready Mix.

That same year, 1966, saw the birth of a new engine, the Maxidyne. It offered a new level of fuel economy and driving ease, with transmission shifting reduced 55 to 65 percent.

The RW Model Super Liner made its entry into the truck market in 1977, and was a big hit with truckers who wanted longer hoods on their conventionals. It was offered for both on-highway and off-highway applications and was originally produced at the Hayward facility. By the late 1970s, Mack had become associated with Renault, the famous French auto maker.

An entirely new truck assembly plant was built in 1987, and billed as the most advanced Class 8 factory ever. Located in Winnsboro, South Carolina, this facility features modular assembly, just-in-time inventory, computerized controls, and the industry's finest painting system.

12,029 of the famous RW Model Super Liner were built, but this model was eventually replaced by the CH Model in 1988. The last of the Super Liners were produced in the spring of 1994, and the final unit was purchased by Yaworski Trucking of Canterbury, Connecticut.

Mack Trucks, Inc. has proven itself as both an innovator and leader in designing and building all kinds of Class 8 trucks, and for this reason, the Bulldog will be around for many years to come.

"Built Like A Mack Truck" is as American an expression as "baseball and hot dogs"–and with good reason.

71

Chapter 13

Marmon Trucks
Built to Work, Made to Last

Marmon Motor Company made its entry into the motor vehicle industry in 1904 in Indianapolis, Indiana. Today Marmon is a division of TIC United Corporation.

Marmon was a pioneer in making top-of-the-line cars. In the first Indianapolis 500, in 1911, a Marmon "Wasp" took first place, winning the race at an incredible speed of 80mph. Marmon was also the first automobile manufacturer to feature a rear-view mirror. The name Marmon ranks with Cadillac, Packard, Pierce Arrow, and other classic automobiles, producing luxury cars powered by V-8, V-12, and V-16 engines. However, the Depression took its toll and Marmon became one of the many car makers to discontinue production of their quality motor cars.

Marmon was quick to answer the challenges brought about by the Second World

Prior to 1970, Marmon trucks were only cab-over models, as seen in this shot from a late 1960s truck show. Back then, the Marmon was looked upon as some sort of hybrid, but today the Marmon name is synonymous with longevity and dependability.

War, coming out with a variety of specialized equipment including half-tracks, heavy equipment hauling apparatus, plane refueling trucks, and other similar vehicles.

In 1963, Marmon was sold to Space, Inc., and moved its facilities to Garland, Texas, where it continued to build trucks. Initially, Marmon built only cab-overs, but by 1970 the company was producing both cab-overs and conventionals.

Marmon, more so than any other truck manufacturer, takes great pride in building trucks that last. Serial number 004 is still in use by its original owner. Another client bought a used Marmon in 1972 and still runs it, putting an average of 100,000 miles on it annually. This customer bought close to twenty more Marmons because of their longevity.

Not only are Marmon trucks becoming more popular in the U.S., but the markets in

The late model Marmon conventional pictured here is a favorite in the owner-operator sector of long distance trucking. More and more "bedbug-haulers" like this one, pulling for Atlas Van Lines, are tired of owning "just another Class 8 big rig" and want something different. Marmon fills this need.

Eastern Europe, the Middle East, Africa, Latin America, and the Far East find that Marmon trucks are meeting their demands.

What makes Marmon different from the competition is that fact that these trucks are not mass-produced . . . each one is built the old fashioned way, one at a time. With only a few hundred employees, Marmon boasts of making its own aluminum cabs and sleepers, as well as making its own chassis and structural members. An average of 550 man-hours goes into the building of each Marmon truck, making this the only truly "hand crafted" Class 8 truck produced in the U.S.

Marmon will continue to be a viable truck manufacturer, satisfying its market of owner-operators, as well as companies engaged in coal production, logging, petroleum hauling, construction, and the military. Marmon recently completed a multi-truck order for the U.S. Air Force. The contract was won by proving that their rigs are tougher, stronger, lighter, and more inexpensive to operate.

Chapter 14

Peterbilt Trucks
Class without Compromise

The first Peterbilt truck was built in 1939, but the beginning of the company is really in 1915 with Frank and William Fageol, who were building luxury cars, trucks, and buses in Oakland, California. Fageol trucks, in the early years, were assembled as conventional trucks using four-cylinder Waukesha gasoline engines.

By 1924 Fageol was a credible builder of trucks and was popular in the logging industry. Because of this success, American Car & Foundry approached the Fageols about building a truck assembly plant in Kent, Ohio, to satisfy an Eastern market for their trucks. The deal turned out to be a bust and in 1929 Fageol was forced into bankruptcy. The Great Depression ruined many businesses, and in 1932 Fageol joined a long list of companies going into receivership. The Waukesha Motor Company and the Central Bank of Oakland assumed control over Fageol.

This comparison photo shows a 1938 Fageol, with the vertical grille, next to a 1939 Peterbilt, with the egg-crate grille. The two have striking similarities.

Even with all of this bad luck, Fageol continued to build many trucks during the 1930s. In 1938 Sterling Motors bought into Fageol, with Sterling soon phasing out Fageol.

Enter T.A. Peterman, a successful lumber and logging entrepreneur from Tacoma, Washington. He took over Fageol/Sterling operations in 1939 for the purpose of building trucks for his own applications in the vast forests of the northwest. Two trucks were built, but the project never fully got rolling.

Nevertheless, this venture put Peterman on solid ground in the trucking industry and was to help pave the way for a much more successful product: Peterbilt trucks.

The transition from Fageol to Peterbilt began in 1939, when fourteen trucks were built. The very first Peterbilts closely resembled the last of the Fageols, and featured an egg-crate grille but with the today's familiar Peterbilt

Seen here in Santa Maria, California, this sharp 1988 Model 379 Peterbilt is owned by Cochiolo Trucking. The Model 379 is a favorite for owner-operators and smaller fleets.

Gene and Hilda Smith of Gridley, California, own El Turbo, a 1949 Peterbilt. This is a *working* truck, and has been featured in trucking magazines all around the World.

This 1956 Model 451 is shown on the back road into Kaiser Steel in Fontana, California, was originally built for Ringsby Truck Lines. Notice the two front steering axles and the drom tank behind the cab. Allyn Tank Lines owned this unit after Ringsby sold it.

script in chrome on the front of each unit. The logo signature was supposed to be Peterman's own signature.

By 1941, Peterbilt had produced a total of eighty-nine trucks and the egg-crate grille give way to a more contemporary-looking front end. Subtle changes were evident in the early 1940s Peterbilts. In late 1944, the style of the logo changed to a rectangular frame surrounding the logo script.

During the war years of the 1940s production had its ups and downs, but by 1945, when T.A. Peterman died, a total of 225 trucks had been built.

Demand for Peterbilt trucks was growing and in 1946 almost 350 big rigs were built. The following year, Peterman's widow sold the company assets, except for the land, and the company name was changed from Peterman Manufacturing Company to Peterbilt Motors Company.

There is some confusion as to exactly when the traditional red oval Peterbilt logo started appearing on the hoods of the trucks. Some put it as early as 1949, while many say that this emblem became standard on all Peterbilt trucks in 1951.

In 1967, the Model 359 was Peterbilt's answer to the wide, tilting hood seen here at Motor Truck Distributors in Los Angeles.

In 1950 the first line of cab-overs was offered by Peterbilt. It was an impressive-looking piece of equipment, and available in both sleeper cab and non-sleeper versions. The cab could be tilted forward but this was not an easy task to perform. The more practical way to access the engine area was to swing the front fenders outward.

1956 saw the second generation cab-over roll off the assembly line. A more refined conventional introduced the previous year was also taking hold.

Peterbilt engineers have always had a "can do" philosophy and could design a truck to suit almost any customer request. The Model 451, which came out in 1956, was specially built to meet the needs of Ringsby Truck Lines of Denver, Colorado. This cab-over unit was equipped with two rear axles and two front steering axles.

In this 1956 photograph, we see a circa 1954 cab-over with a drom box behind the sleeper cab. Joe Cabral, dba L.A.-Eureka Lines ran this truck up and down California.

Next page
Cliff Wilkins of Blackwell, Oklahoma owns this show-horse –a 1966 Peterbilt sporting a 314in wheelbase. The hood was extended 15in and the sleeper was home-built. It took three years to fully complete this restoration.

Dick Smith ran this 1969 Peterbilt truck and trailer, hauling cattle for Great Western Packing Co., of Vernon, California. A 318hp Detroit Diesel pulled up to forty-eight head of "fat" cattle. This rig traveled the highways and backroads of Imperial Valley and the Bakersfield/Fresno area of California.

It came with a standard sleeper cab or with a penthouse sleeper, located above the driver. This design was new to Peterbilt but the folks at White Freightliner had been making a penthouse sleeper available for several years for truck and trailer applications.

In 1958, Peterbilt became part of the Paccar family, which also owns Kenworth. With Paccar finances, a new factory was built in Newark, California. This new plant became fully operational in 1960 and production rose sharply through the 1960s to a total of 21,000 units built.

A second assembly facility opened its doors in 1969 in Nashville, Tennessee. 72,000 vehicles bearing the name Peterbilt, were built at both plants by the close of the 1970s.

At about the time that the Nashville plant opened, Peterbilt introduced the 110in cab-over. This was a direct challenge to White Freightliner, who had offered the same model several years before anyone else. This larger cab is still a popular model. Peterbilt was so successful that, in 1980, a third assembly plant was built in Denton, Texas.

In 1981 the famous Model 352 cab-over was being phased out for the current Model 362. This model's looks changed completely. It sported a one-piece flat windshield, although a two-piece was also available.

Peterbilt ceased production at the Newark plant in 1986, although engineering and product development continued at this location for a few more years.

Floyd Rogers of Puyallup, Washington was one of the last truckers to run a full-box truck and trailer conventional produce rig on the west coast with this 1969 Peterbilt. This particular set up was popular in the 1940s and 1950s but became obsolete with more liberal length laws. Note that the sleeper is built into the produce body directly behind the cab.

In 1988 a new, more aerodynamic cab-over hit the highways in the form of the Model 372, nicknamed the "Winnebago." Though this model can be seen running the Interstates, the Model 362 seems to have a greater acceptance.

Peterbilt may have gotten off to somewhat of a rocky start, but T.A. Peterman would be proud to see his signature on so many Class 8 trucks, both on and off the highway. Today, Peterbilt trucks can be found in all parts of the World.

Peterbilt, more than any other truck, has enjoyed unsurpassed popularity with both owner-operators and the larger fleets, as evidenced by the overall resale value of used Peterbilts. It is therefore obvious that "Peterbilt" and "Class" are synonymous.

The 1983 Model 362 is seen here at a dairy in Chino, California. Set up as a truck and trailer, this 73in sleeper cab rig is owned by Ed Erro, who has been hauling hay and alfalfa in California and Nevada for over thirty years.

Chapter 15

Sterling Trucks

Gone But Not Forgotten

The Sterling was famous for its motorcycle-type of front fenders, oak-lined frames with bolted crossmembers, and redefining the importance of chain-driven vehicles. But in order to appreciate this company, we need to start from the beginning.

William M. Sternberg began the Sternberg Manufacturing Company in West Allis, a suburb of Milwaukee, Wisconsin in 1907. Right from its start, the Sternberg trucks were innovative, building right-hand drive trucks ranging from one to five tons with most models in the cab-over configuration.

By 1914, their chain-driven trucks had become an accepted part of trucking. However, their line now featured the bonneted hood, that is, the engine located in front of the cab, with the exception of its seven-ton model which remained still a cab-over.

Most of Sterling's production of Class 8 trucks in the early 1940s went to the U.S. Navy. This 1942 model is powered by a 150hp Cummins diesel engine. Rear tires are the original from 1942 . . . notice the chaindrive near rear tires. Sterling was famous for its use of chaindrive trucks.

It was also during 1914 that the company's name changed from Sternberg Manufacturing Company to Sterling Motor Truck Company. This was due primarily to increasing anti-German sentiment as World War I approached the U.S.

With the onset of the First World War, Sterling was one of several truck makers called upon to build the "Liberty" Class B, three-to five-ton transport trucks for the military. Sterling was able to build 479 of these and many remained in use after the war.

By the 1920s, Sterling was getting its share of the truck market and in 1924 built a popular six-speed, five-ton model that was, of course, chain-driven. Sterling continued to prosper and in 1928, Sterling merged with the Corbitt Truck Company of Henderson, North Carolina. Sterling became the parent company while Corbitt continued to

This 1952 Sterling-White is owned by Bill Maynard of
Valley Center, California. It has a 165hp Cummins engine
with a five and three transmission.

Here is a 1951 Sterling-White, the first year of the nameplate change. This rig was originally one of many pulling for Western Truck Lines. Pictured here, it was owned by Frank and Ruth Tally of Alhambra, California. The tractor had a Cummins 220hp diesel, backed by a five-speed main and a three-speed auxiliary transmission.

operate independently, building Class 8 trucks into the 1950s. By 1929 Sterling offered eleven different models, all of which were chain-driven.

At this time, research was on-going in the use of aluminum in the fabrication of trucks and truck bodies. In 1930 Sterling, together with Heil Body Company, offered a three-axle dump truck, using an aluminum Heil dump body on a Class 8 chain-drive truck known as the DC26. The DC26 weighed in over 2,000lb lighter than its steel counterpart.

When other truck makers were feeling the affects of the Great Depression, Sterling was continued to enjoy prosperity. In 1932 Sterling bought out LaFrance-Republic Sales Corp. of Alma, Michigan, whose assets were transferred to the Sterling facility in Milwaukee. 1932 also brought Sterling into association with Cummins Diesel and the diesel engine was now available in Sterlings from four-ton models on up.

The following year, Sterling reintroduced the cab-over with the "Camel Back" model. To access the engine, the cab was tilted back making it easier for the engine to be serviced. By 1935 the Camel Back's cab remained basically the same as earlier models, but now the cab now tilted forward to access the engine compartment.

In 1938 Sterling acquired the Fageol Truck & Coach Company of Oakland, California, who was the forerunner of Peterbilt. By 1939 Fageol had ceased production, but Sterling continued to maintain a large inventory of Fageol parts.

In 1940, Sterling placed more of its emphasis on driver comfort. Naugahyde, which was flexible and resisted cracking, was used to upholster the interior.

Sterling was still producing civilian trucks when World War II broke out and built a total of 544 rigs in 1944. However, most of the trucks they built during the war years went to the U.S. Navy in the form of cargo trucks, tractors for pulling low-bed trailers, and ten-ton wreckers. The years after the war saw Sterling continue to make inroads, particularly in California and New England.

In 1950, Sterling came out with another cab-over, possibly to compete with the bullnose Kenworth. The TG model cab-over came with an adjustable steering wheel, enabling the driver to lock the steering wheel into any of four positions. In June of 1951, the White Motor Company of Cleveland, Ohio, took over Sterling. Soon after, all nameplates bore the name Sterling-White. For all intents and purposes, the last Sterling-White was produced in 1953, although a few were built in 1954 and Sterling-White appeared on some mobile cranes that were built up to 1958.

In its forty-six year life, Sterling produced a total of 12,000 trucks. One thing that made Sterling a viable competitor was its vast network of factory branches and dealerships across the country.

Sterlings were rugged and built to last. Some old-timers will tell you that you "aimed" a Sterling; not simply drove it. Looking out through its strange-looking windshield, you could see the front fenders flapping like the wings of some great bird.

Chapter 16

Western Star Trucks
Canadian Made

Western Star Trucks are relatively new, as opposed to the majority of truck manufacturers who got their start around the turn of the century. Western Star was established in 1967 as the Canadian subsidiary of the White Motor Corporation of Cleveland, Ohio. Both production and engineering for Western Star is located in Kelowna, British Columbia.

In 1981, following the sale of the U.S. based White Motor Corp. to Volvo of Sweden, the Western Star division of White was sold to two Canadian resource companies, and thus Western Star was on its own.

Western Star always enjoyed a kind of independent existence and today is no different. Ninety-three percent of all staff work is performed in Canada, where one hundred percent of all production takes place.

Negotiating a wide turn, a 1989 Western Star is seen here operating for the Metropolitan Water District of Southern California. State and local governmental departments recognize the need for a custom built truck for certain applications. Western Star offers over 4,000 options on the five models that they produce, making it a much sought after truck to own and operate.

At one time, Western Star made both cab-overs as well as conventional models, however, but in more recent times the cab-over has been phased.

With five different models available, Western Star offers over 4,000 options in both right-and left-hand drive. Because of this flexibility, Western Star units are popular in over twenty countries, throughout the World.

Currently, approximately forty-six percent of all Western Star's sales remain in Canada, while an additional forty-three percent of sales go south of the border into the U.S. Finally, eleven percent of truck sales go to other countries.

Western Star trucks are custom-built to meet even the most severe challenges offered both by man and nature in any part of the world.

Much of Western Star's success can be found in trucks owned by individual truckers, like this black beauty, fully dressed out for on-highway application. While the larger fleets see little need for chrome frills, it is the owner-operators who really set the stage for positive public acceptance.

Typical applications are as follows: highway freight haulage, forty-three percent; logging, mining, oil field, thirty percent; construction, twenty-one percent; other, six percent.

Future plans for Western Star include the construction of a new cab plant, expansion and updating of current facilities, enlargement of the present offices, the introduction of both a new cab as well as a new sleeper, and the continued expansion into foreign markets.

Although Western Star may be "a late bloomer," in the Class 8 trucks arena, their reputation as a builder of both strong and reliable trucks has been established . . . ask any owner or driver.

The 1989 Western Star slopenose is their version of the ant-eater.

Chapter 17

White Trucks

Its Popularity Continues

The history of White can be traced back to 1859, when Thomas Howard White, along with George Baker and D'Arcy Porter, formed a company, the White Manufacturing Company and began making hand-operated sewing machines in Templeton, Massachusetts. In 1866, the company moved its operations to Cleveland, Ohio, and continued making sewing machines, which sold for ten dollars. Ten years later the company expanded to make paraffin lamps, roller skates, and bicycles. The company was so successful at building bicycles that by the 1890s White considered building automobiles.

Around 1900, three of the founder's four sons embarked on automobile manufacturing venture. Thomas White lent support in the form of production expertise and capital. The first White car, like many that followed, was steam-powered.

Seen here at a Virginia truck stop, is a WC series with integral sleeper, circa 1959. This model was a popular rig with truckers in the southeastern part of the U.S.

About fifty cars were built by White in 1900 called "Stanhopes." Included in that number were White's first two commercial rigs, which were pie wagons.

By 1906 White was a recognized leader in the production of steam-driven cars; his production total was 1,534 vehicles. From 1909 to 1910, White built steam powered vehicles as well as gasoline, but the steam engine was being phased out in favor of the more popular gasoline engine. By 1911 White was building gasoline-powered engines exclusively.

White built commercial vehicles such as ambulances, buses, and fire engines with pneumatic tires.

With the outbreak of World War One, the U.S. Army chose White as their standard truck. A total of 18,000 White trucks of various body configurations were built and saw action in

This 1986 Volvo-White with integral sleeper is owned by Jim Bronte. This unit was originally owned by PST Vans of Salt Lake City, and is used daily to haul freight.

Europe. Some of these were used on the home-front for training purposes.

By the war's end, White had phased out the automobile division and dedicated itself to producing trucks with universal driveshafts instead of chain-drives. White's first special bus chassis was assembled in 1921 and air brakes became available a few years later. 1928 saw the Model 59 introduced. This was a conventional truck with a payload of three to four tons, and was also the first truck with a six-cylinder engine. By 1930, White was building larger, three-axle trucks capable of carrying ten tons.

The Depression forced many truck manufacturers into receivership or bankruptcy.

White was able to take over one of those victims, The Indiana Truck Company, and move its operations to Cleveland.

In 1934, White introduced the 730 series, which was a cab-over equipped with a twelve-cylinder engine. It was not their most popular model, but it did set the stage for future cab-overs with six-cylinder engines.

During the mid-1930s, aerodynamic design was becoming an important factor in truck design. In the late 1930s, White called upon Count Alexis de Saknoffsky to design the now-famous Labatt's Beer truck, featuring a White cab-over Model 818 and matching aerodynamic trailer. This stunning truck was delivered to the brewer in 1937.

Although not technically a Class 8 truck, this Model 3000 with sleeper cab illustrates the aerodynamics of this cab-over, perhaps one of White's most popular trucks.

By the following year, White had introduced the "Superpower," a new generation of side-valve gasoline engines which were popular up into the 1950s, when the name was changed to the "Mustang."

With the onset of World War II, White was called upon to supply rigs for military use. Some were intended for standard trucking applications, while others were designed as armored-cars and half-tracks. The latter saw plenty of action and received much acclaim.

Many of these trucks are still being used in many parts of the world.

Not all of White's production was destined for military use. The WA series came out in 1940, and replaced the 700 and 800 series of the 1930s. The WB series appeared after the war and was basically unchanged, except for a new cab ventilation system.

In 1949 White came out with the WC series, and although it had the same general appearance as previous models, it had a couple of popular options. It was available with either a gas or diesel-powered engine and the option of an integral sleeper cab. This model was a particular favorite with the nation's long distance van line operators, or "bedbug-haulers," as well as J.H. Rose Truck Lines, a large oil field hauler operating out of Texas.

While the interior of this model was extremely cramped, greater payloads could be carried. This was continually an issue in the 1940s and 1950s as length laws were quite restrictive.

At about the same time that the WC series was introduced, still another dramatic model was to premier . . . the 3000! This cab-over was more driver-friendly, and like the W series, offered an integral sleeper for transcontinental trucking. The 3000 offered gasoline or diesel power. The 3000 seemed to defy time, but was phased out because its aerodynamic cab was simply too expensive to produce.

In 1957, White bought Reo Motors primarily to acquire Reo's overhead valve (OHV) gasoline engine. This was to replace the famous "Mustang" engine, which was renamed the "Super Mustang." The following year, White purchased Diamond T. Reo and Diamond T were merged and marketed jointly under the name of Diamond Reo.

The White 5000 series came out in 1959 and was an unusual looking truck to say the least. This model proved to be somewhat of a failure in terms of quality, function, and sales. The cab featured fiberglass construction, which had little impact resistance in collisions. Its ill-fitting doors also allowed rain water to leak in. The Model 5000 was produced only until 1962, when it was replaced by the Model 7000.

The 7000 was fabricated of aluminum, which was much cheaper to build and repair. This model was particularly well received in the Midwest and Eastern U.S. It was available with either a sleeper or non-sleeper cab, and was affectionately referred to as "The Japanese Freightliner," by many operators.

The Road Commander became available in 1972, and was much more refined by 1975. It was the first member of the "New Family" of trucks offered by White.

Jumping back a little, 1966 saw the new conventionals in the form of the series 4000 and 9000, featuring an Autocar cab as standard equipment and a redesigned fiberglass tilting front end.

In the 1960s and early 1970s, White still believed that there was a market for gasoline-powered engines, and as a result had purchased Cummins diesel engines and converted them into gasoline engines. These new engines were sold under the names "Mustang VIII," and "White Giesel," which stood for gasoline/diesel. This venture proved to be a disaster for White, as the Environmental Protection Agency (EPA) had begun to enforce stringent air pollution and engine emission regulations. Soon after, White would join other Class 8 truck manufacturers by relying on outside vendors to supply drivetrain components for their trucks.

In 1975, a new factory was built and the company moved from Cleveland to New River

The 5000 series White used fiberglass in the construction of its cab. The truck suffered serious problems, as the cab leaked in the rain, doors did not fit well, and had no impact resistance in collisions.

Valley, Virginia. Another new plant was built in Orrville, Ohio, to produce cabs for the New Family of trucks. The models in the New Family were phased in over several years, beginning with the Road Commander 2 in 1975, the Road Expeditor in 1976, the Road Boss 2 in 1977, and the Autocar Construcktor 2 in 1978. All were well received, with the exceptions of the Road Boss 2 and the Autocar Construcktor 2.

1980 was especially important, as it spelled the downfall of this corporate giant. Perhaps it was White's over-expansion, or the rise of interest rates, or the deregulation of trucking. For whatever reason, White fell on hard times and filed for Chapter 11 under U.S. Federal Law.

On August 31, 1981, the newly formed Volvo-White Corporation took over the trucks

Seen here in 1967, a 7000 series, better known as "The Japanese Freightliner," is outfitted with a sleeper cab. This truck was operated by Becker's Transport of Kenilworth, New Jersey.

This Road Commander, circa 1973, is being pulled over by the California Highway Patrol. Many Road Commanders can still be seen hauling in various parts of the country.

being produced by White Motor Corporation. It was the start of a new era for White. The New Family of trucks was backed by the financial strength of a new company, and truck sales, which had been on a downward slide, began to climb.

In 1988, General Motors became part of the New Family. GM had phased out its "General," a truck that had proven to be popular rig all over America. GM continues to build Class 7 and smaller trucks with great success.

With the additional capital of GM, the current New Family of Class 8 trucks includes Volvo, White, GM, and Autocar. Barring any unforeseen calamities, this family of truck builders will be making many more big rigs, producing the kinds of Class 8 trucks needed for the twenty-first century.

Index

American Car & Foundry, 74
American Coleman, 8, 9
Anderson, W.E., 46
Autocar, 10-13, 95

Baker, George, 90
bobtail (defined), 11
Brockway Carriage Factory, 14
Brockway, 17
Brockway, William, N., 14, 17

cab-over (defined), 10
Case-Tenneco, 54
Chrysler Corporation, 224
Chrysler, Walter, 24, 25
Clarke, John S., 10
Clarke, Louis S., 10
class 8 (defined), 11
Consolidated Freightways, 34
conventional (defined), 10
Corbitt Truck Company, 82

Daimler-Benz, 38
Diamond Reo, 23
Diamond T Motor Company, 18
Diamond T, 18-20, 23
Dodge, 24, 255
Dodge Brothers, 24, 25
Durant, William, C., 40

Fageol, Frank, 74
Fageol, William, 74
Fageol Truck & Coach Company, 85
Finn, Barney, 40, 45
Ford, Henry, 28
Ford Motor Company, 28, 29
Freightliner Corporation, 34-38
Freightways Manufacturing Company, 34, 35

Gearmatic Co. Ltd., 47
General Motors Company (GMC), 40, 41, 44, 45
General Motors Corporation, 40
General Motors, 12, 95
Grabowsky, Max, 40
Grabowsky, Morris, 40
Grabowsky Motor Vehicle Company, 40
Graham Brothers, 24, 25

Hayes, Douglas, 46
Hayes Mfg. Co. Ltd., 46
Hayes, 47
Hayes-Anderson Motor Co. Ltd., 46
H.R.L., 56

Indiana Truck Corporation, 14
International Auto-Buggy, 48
International Harvester, 20, 23, 48
International Harvester/Navistar, 48-50, 54

Johnston, E.A., 48

Kenworth (KW), 56, 57, 62-65

LaFrance-Republic Sales Corp., 85
Lawrence Manufacturing, 46

Mack, Augustus, 66
Mack Brothers Wagon Works, 66
Mack, John, 66
Mack Trucks, 47, 66, 68, 71
Marmon Motor Company, 72, 73
Marx, Albert, 40, 45
Maxwell Motor Company, 24

Navistar, 48
New Diamond T Company, 23

Olds, Ransom, 24
Osterlund Incorporated, 23

Pacific Car & Foundry (Paccar), 27, 32, 57, 47, 80
Peterbilt, 74, 77, 80, 81
Peterman Manufacturing Company, 77
Peterman, T.A., 74, 77, 81
Pittsburgh Motor Vehicle Company, 10
Porter, D'Arcy, 90

Renault, 71

Saknoffsky, Count Alexis de., 91
semi (defined), 11
Space, Inc., 72
Sterling Motor Truck Company, 82, 85
Sterling-White, 85
Sternberg Manufacturing Company, 82
Sternberg, William, M., 82
straight truck (defined), 11

TIC United Corporation, 72
Tilt, Charles, A., 18, 23

Volvo, 86, 95
Volvo-White Truck Corporation, 12, 45, 94
Vulcan, 56

Waukesha Motor Company, 74
Western Star Trucks, 86, 89
White Manufacturing Company, 90
White Motor Company, 11, 14, 23, 37, 85
White Motor Corporation, 12, 86, 90-95
White's New Family, 12, 45, 94, 95
White Reo Motors, 93
White-GMC-Autocar, 12
White, Thomas, Howard, 90

Yellow Cab Manufacturing Company, 40

Focus On

Reducing and Calculating Fractions

KUMON

Improper Fractions and Mixed Numbers

date / / score /100

1 Write the missing number in each box below. A–E are improper fractions and a–d are mixed numbers.

4 points per box

①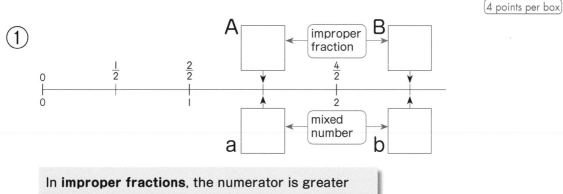

In **improper fractions**, the numerator is greater than or equal to the denominator. A **mixed number** consists of a whole number and a proper fraction (the numerator is smaller than the denominator).

②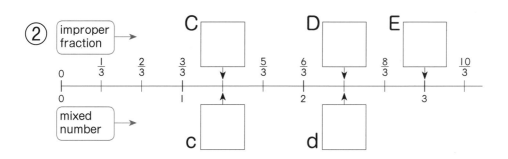

Fractions that are equal to whole numbers, for example $1 = \frac{3}{3}$, $2 = \frac{6}{3}$, can be divided like so: $3 \div 3 = 1$, $6 \div 3 = 2$.

2 Change the improper fractions into whole numbers or mixed numbers by dividing the improper fractions as shown. Write the appropriate number in each box below.

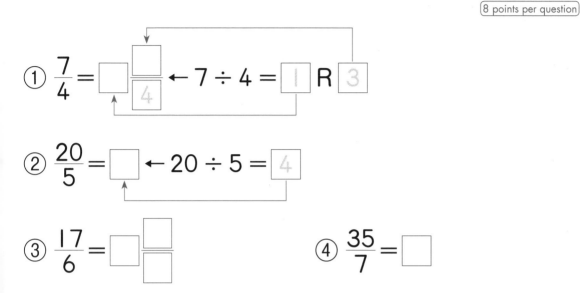

① $\dfrac{7}{4} = \boxed{}\dfrac{\boxed{}}{4} \leftarrow 7 \div 4 = \boxed{1}\ \text{R}\ \boxed{3}$

② $\dfrac{20}{5} = \boxed{} \leftarrow 20 \div 5 = \boxed{4}$

③ $\dfrac{17}{6} = \boxed{}\dfrac{\boxed{}}{\boxed{}}$

④ $\dfrac{35}{7} = \boxed{}$

3 Change the mixed numbers into improper fractions by calculating the mixed numbers as shown. Write the appropriate numbers in each box below.

① $3\dfrac{1}{2} = \dfrac{\boxed{}}{2} \leftarrow 2 \times 3 + 1 = \boxed{7}$

② $1\dfrac{3}{5} = \dfrac{\boxed{}}{5} \leftarrow 5 \times 1 + 3 = \boxed{8}$

③ $2\dfrac{2}{7} = \dfrac{\boxed{}}{\boxed{}}$

④ $3\dfrac{5}{8} = \dfrac{\boxed{}}{\boxed{}}$

1 Write the appropriate number in each box below.

7 points per question

① $\dfrac{3}{5} + \dfrac{1}{5} = \dfrac{\square}{5}$ (3+1)

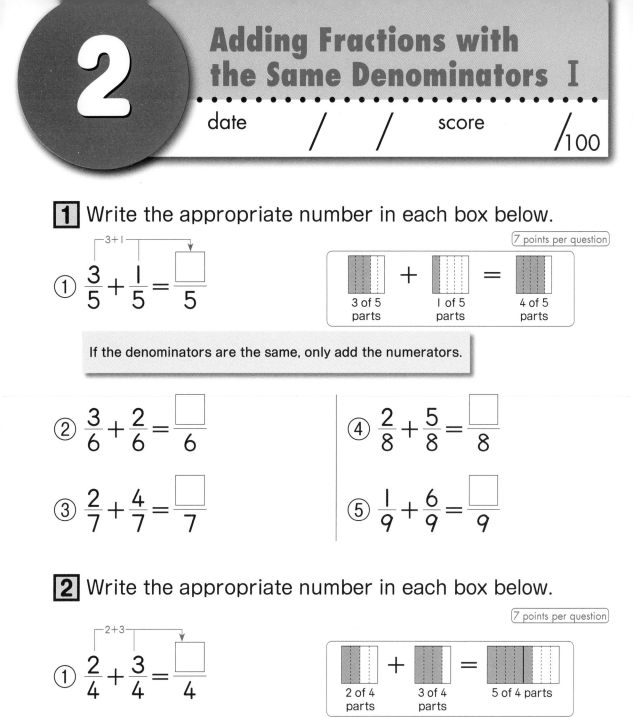

+ =

3 of 5 parts   1 of 5 parts   4 of 5 parts

If the denominators are the same, only add the numerators.

② $\dfrac{3}{6} + \dfrac{2}{6} = \dfrac{\square}{6}$

③ $\dfrac{2}{7} + \dfrac{4}{7} = \dfrac{\square}{7}$

④ $\dfrac{2}{8} + \dfrac{5}{8} = \dfrac{\square}{8}$

⑤ $\dfrac{1}{9} + \dfrac{6}{9} = \dfrac{\square}{9}$

2 Write the appropriate number in each box below.

7 points per question

① $\dfrac{2}{4} + \dfrac{3}{4} = \dfrac{\square}{4}$ (2+3)

+ =

2 of 4 parts   3 of 4 parts   5 of 4 parts

$= \square\dfrac{\square}{4}$

If the answer is an improper fraction, change it to a mixed number.

② $\dfrac{2}{3} + \dfrac{2}{3} = \dfrac{\square}{3} = \square\dfrac{\square}{3}$

3 Write the appropriate number in each box below.

7 points per question

① $\dfrac{1}{3} + \dfrac{2}{3} = \dfrac{\boxed{}}{3}$

$= \boxed{}$

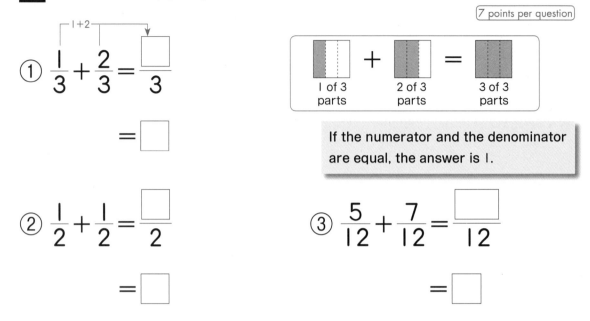

If the numerator and the denominator are equal, the answer is 1.

② $\dfrac{1}{2} + \dfrac{1}{2} = \dfrac{\boxed{}}{2}$

$= \boxed{}$

③ $\dfrac{5}{12} + \dfrac{7}{12} = \dfrac{\boxed{}}{12}$

$= \boxed{}$

4 Answer the questions below. Then change any answers that are the improper fractions into mixed numbers.

6 points per question

Be careful not to add the denominators like $\dfrac{1}{3} + \dfrac{1}{3} \neq \dfrac{2}{6}$ at ①. You must only add the numerators and keep the denominators as is.

① $\dfrac{1}{3} + \dfrac{1}{3} =$

② $\dfrac{3}{6} + \dfrac{4}{6} =$

③ $\dfrac{4}{5} + \dfrac{1}{5} =$

④ $\dfrac{6}{7} + \dfrac{5}{7} =$

⑤ $\dfrac{9}{10} + \dfrac{4}{10} =$

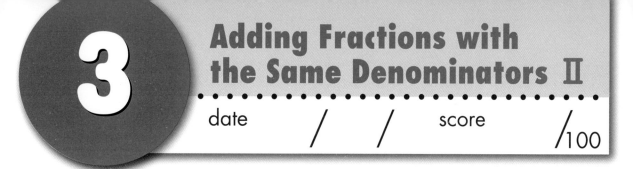

Adding Fractions with the Same Denominators II

date / / score /100

1 Write the appropriate number in each box below.

6 points per question

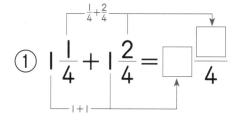

① $1\dfrac{1}{4} + 1\dfrac{2}{4} = \boxed{}\dfrac{\boxed{}}{4}$

Add each part separately—add whole numbers together, and then add fractions together.

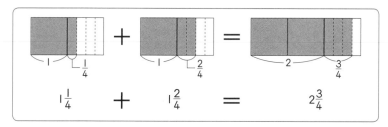

② $4\dfrac{1}{3} + 3\dfrac{1}{3} = \boxed{}\dfrac{\boxed{}}{3}$

③ $3\dfrac{2}{5} + 1\dfrac{1}{5} = \boxed{}\dfrac{\boxed{}}{5}$

④ $1\dfrac{2}{6} + 1\dfrac{3}{6} = \boxed{}\dfrac{\boxed{}}{6}$

⑤ $1\dfrac{2}{7} + 2\dfrac{3}{7} = \boxed{}\dfrac{\boxed{}}{7}$

⑥ $1\dfrac{1}{9} + 2\dfrac{7}{9} = \boxed{}\dfrac{\boxed{}}{9}$

©Kumon Publishing Co., Ltd.

2 Write the appropriate number in each box below.

(8 points per question)

① $2\frac{3}{5} + \frac{1}{5} = \boxed{2}\frac{\boxed{}}{5}$

$\frac{3}{5}+\frac{1}{5}$

② $3\frac{3}{8} + \frac{2}{8} = \boxed{}\frac{\boxed{}}{8}$

③ $\frac{4}{9} + 1\frac{1}{9} = \boxed{}\frac{\boxed{}}{9}$

④ $\frac{3}{10} + 2\frac{4}{10} = \boxed{}\frac{\boxed{}}{10}$

3 Write the appropriate number in each box below.

(8 points per question)

① $3 + 2\frac{5}{6} = \boxed{}\frac{\boxed{5}}{6}$

3+2

② $4 + 2\frac{1}{2} = \boxed{}\frac{\boxed{}}{2}$

Add each part separately—add
whole numbers together, and
then add fractions together.

③ $1\frac{2}{3} + 5 = \boxed{}\frac{\boxed{}}{3}$

④ $3\frac{3}{4} + 2 = \boxed{}\frac{\boxed{}}{4}$

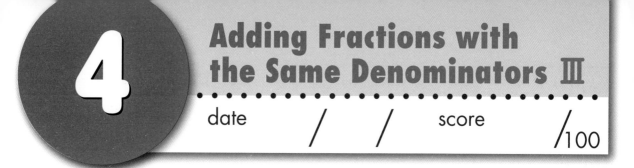

1 Write the appropriate number in each box below.

10 points per question

① $1\frac{2}{4}+1\frac{3}{4}=\boxed{2}\frac{\boxed{5}}{4}=\boxed{3}\frac{\boxed{1}}{4}$

> If the answer includes an improper fraction, convert it to a mixed number and add the whole numbers together. In this case, $2\frac{5}{4}=3\frac{1}{4}$, so the correct answer is $3\frac{1}{4}$.

② $1\frac{2}{3}+1\frac{2}{3}=2\frac{\boxed{}}{3}=3\frac{\boxed{}}{3}$

③ $2\frac{4}{5}+1\frac{3}{5}=3\frac{\boxed{}}{5}=4\frac{\boxed{}}{5}$

④ $3\frac{5}{6}+1\frac{2}{6}=4\frac{\boxed{}}{6}=\boxed{}\frac{\boxed{}}{6}$

⑤ $1\frac{4}{7}+3\frac{6}{7}=4\frac{\boxed{}}{7}=\boxed{}\frac{\boxed{}}{7}$

⑥ $2\frac{6}{9}+2\frac{8}{9}=4\frac{\boxed{}}{9}=\boxed{}\frac{\boxed{}}{9}$

2 Write the appropriate number in each box below.

5 points per question

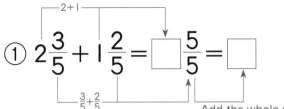

① $2\frac{3}{5} + 1\frac{2}{5} = \boxed{}\frac{5}{5} = \boxed{}$

Add the whole numbers if the fraction equals an improper fraction.

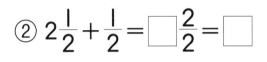

② $2\frac{1}{2} + \frac{1}{2} = \boxed{}\frac{2}{2} = \boxed{}$

If the numerator and the denominator are the same, the fraction equals 1.

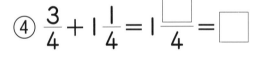

③ $\frac{2}{3} + 1\frac{1}{3} = \boxed{}\frac{3}{3} = \boxed{}$

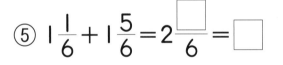

④ $\frac{3}{4} + 1\frac{1}{4} = 1\frac{\boxed{}}{4} = \boxed{}$

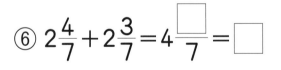

⑤ $1\frac{1}{6} + 1\frac{5}{6} = 2\frac{\boxed{}}{6} = \boxed{}$

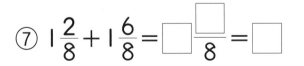

⑥ $2\frac{4}{7} + 2\frac{3}{7} = 4\frac{\boxed{}}{7} = \boxed{}$

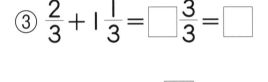

⑦ $1\frac{2}{8} + 1\frac{6}{8} = \boxed{}\frac{\boxed{}}{8} = \boxed{}$

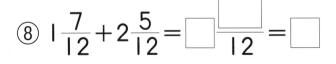

⑧ $1\frac{7}{12} + 2\frac{5}{12} = \boxed{}\frac{\boxed{}}{12} = \boxed{}$

1 Write the appropriate number in each box below.

5 points per question

① $\dfrac{4}{5} - \dfrac{3}{5} = \dfrac{\square}{5}$ (4−3)

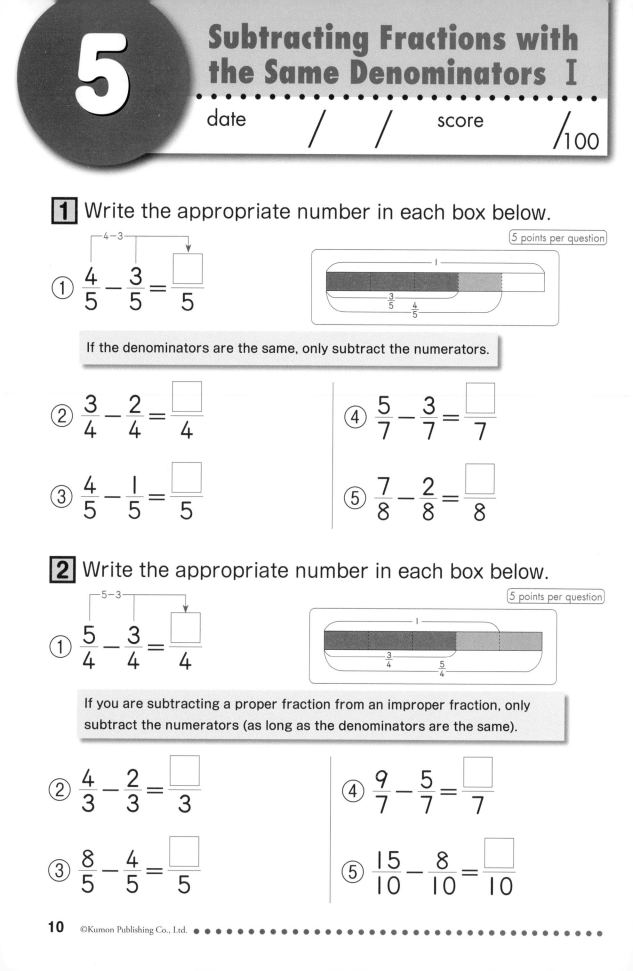

If the denominators are the same, only subtract the numerators.

② $\dfrac{3}{4} - \dfrac{2}{4} = \dfrac{\square}{4}$

③ $\dfrac{4}{5} - \dfrac{1}{5} = \dfrac{\square}{5}$

④ $\dfrac{5}{7} - \dfrac{3}{7} = \dfrac{\square}{7}$

⑤ $\dfrac{7}{8} - \dfrac{2}{8} = \dfrac{\square}{8}$

2 Write the appropriate number in each box below.

5 points per question

① $\dfrac{5}{4} - \dfrac{3}{4} = \dfrac{\square}{4}$ (5−3)

If you are subtracting a proper fraction from an improper fraction, only subtract the numerators (as long as the denominators are the same).

② $\dfrac{4}{3} - \dfrac{2}{3} = \dfrac{\square}{3}$

③ $\dfrac{8}{5} - \dfrac{4}{5} = \dfrac{\square}{5}$

④ $\dfrac{9}{7} - \dfrac{5}{7} = \dfrac{\square}{7}$

⑤ $\dfrac{15}{10} - \dfrac{8}{10} = \dfrac{\square}{10}$

3 Write the appropriate number in each box below.

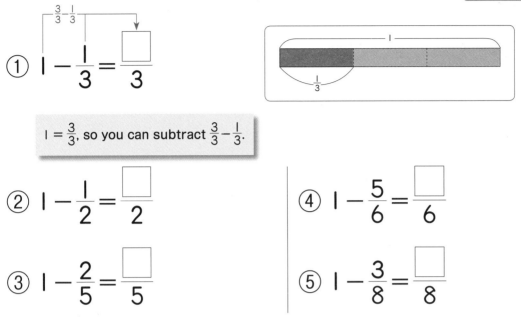

① $1 - \dfrac{1}{3} = \dfrac{\Box}{3}$

$1 = \dfrac{3}{3}$, so you can subtract $\dfrac{3}{3} - \dfrac{1}{3}$.

② $1 - \dfrac{1}{2} = \dfrac{\Box}{2}$

③ $1 - \dfrac{2}{5} = \dfrac{\Box}{5}$

④ $1 - \dfrac{5}{6} = \dfrac{\Box}{6}$

⑤ $1 - \dfrac{3}{8} = \dfrac{\Box}{8}$

4 Answer the questions below. Hint: you do not have to change improper fractions to proper fractions in order to calculate the answer.

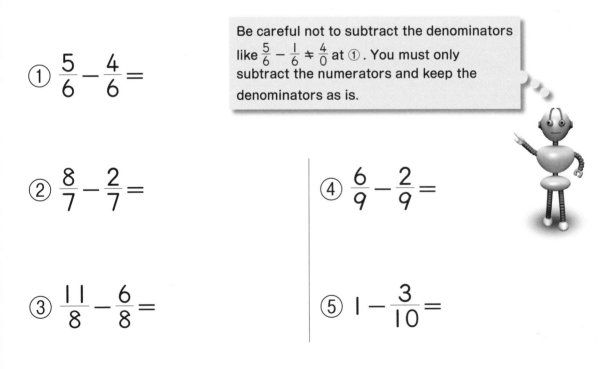

Be careful not to subtract the denominators like $\dfrac{5}{6} - \dfrac{1}{6} \neq \dfrac{4}{0}$ at ①. You must only subtract the numerators and keep the denominators as is.

① $\dfrac{5}{6} - \dfrac{4}{6} =$

② $\dfrac{8}{7} - \dfrac{2}{7} =$

③ $\dfrac{11}{8} - \dfrac{6}{8} =$

④ $\dfrac{6}{9} - \dfrac{2}{9} =$

⑤ $1 - \dfrac{3}{10} =$

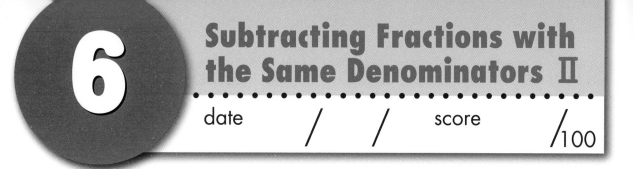

1 Write the appropriate number in each box below.

5 points per question

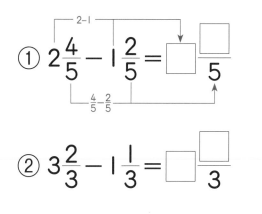

① $2\dfrac{4}{5} - 1\dfrac{2}{5} = \boxed{}\dfrac{\boxed{}}{5}$

Subtract each part separately—subtract whole numbers, and then subtract fractions.

② $3\dfrac{2}{3} - 1\dfrac{1}{3} = \boxed{}\dfrac{\boxed{}}{3}$

③ $3\dfrac{4}{7} - 1\dfrac{2}{7} = \boxed{}\dfrac{\boxed{}}{7}$

2 Write the appropriate number in each box below.

5 points per question

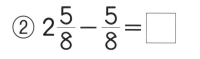

① $3\dfrac{3}{4} - \dfrac{2}{4} = \boxed{3}\dfrac{\boxed{}}{4}$

In ①, subtract the fractions but keep the whole number.

② $2\dfrac{5}{8} - \dfrac{5}{8} = \boxed{}$

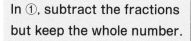

$\dfrac{5}{8} - \dfrac{5}{8} = 0$ in ②, so the answer is the remaining whole number.

③ $1\dfrac{5}{12} - \dfrac{4}{12} = \boxed{}\dfrac{\boxed{}}{12}$

3 Write the appropriate number in each box below.

① $4\dfrac{1}{2} - 3 = \boxed{}\dfrac{\boxed{}}{2}$

Subtract the whole numbers but keep the fraction.

② $4\dfrac{3}{5} - 2 = \boxed{}\dfrac{\boxed{}}{5}$

③ $3\dfrac{1}{3} - 3 = \dfrac{\boxed{}}{3}$

The answer to ③ is the fraction alone.

4 Subtract.

① $3\dfrac{1}{2} - 2 =$

⑤ $5\dfrac{5}{9} - \dfrac{4}{9} =$

② $2\dfrac{5}{6} - 2\dfrac{4}{6} =$

⑥ $2\dfrac{8}{10} - \dfrac{5}{10} =$

③ $4\dfrac{6}{7} - \dfrac{3}{7} =$

⑦ $5\dfrac{9}{11} - 3 =$

When you finish, check your answers. Then correct your mistakes by trying the question again.

④ $2\dfrac{6}{8} - 1\dfrac{1}{8} =$

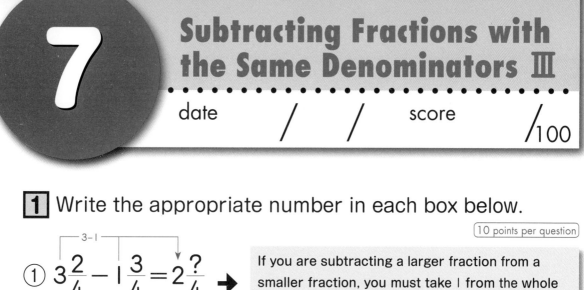

1 Write the appropriate number in each box below.

10 points per question

① $3\dfrac{2}{4} - 1\dfrac{3}{4} = 2\dfrac{?}{4}$

┌─ 3−1 ─┐

We can not subtract $\dfrac{3}{4}$ from $\dfrac{2}{4}$.

If you are subtracting a larger fraction from a smaller fraction, you must take 1 from the whole number to make the smaller fraction large enough.

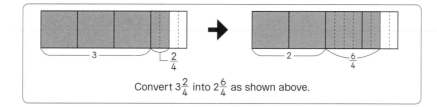

Convert $3\dfrac{2}{4}$ into $2\dfrac{6}{4}$ as shown above.

Move 1 from the whole number.

$$3\dfrac{2}{4} - 1\dfrac{3}{4} = 2\dfrac{6}{4} - 1\dfrac{3}{4}$$

$$= \boxed{}\dfrac{\boxed{}}{4}$$

② $2\dfrac{1}{3} - 1\dfrac{2}{3} = 1\dfrac{\boxed{}}{3} - 1\dfrac{2}{3} = \dfrac{\boxed{}}{3}$

③ $4\dfrac{2}{5} - 1\dfrac{3}{5} = 3\dfrac{\boxed{}}{5} - 1\dfrac{3}{5}$

$$= \boxed{}\dfrac{\boxed{}}{5}$$

2 Subtract.

① $4\dfrac{3}{5} - 2\dfrac{4}{5} =$

② $3\dfrac{2}{6} - 1\dfrac{3}{6} =$

③ $1\dfrac{3}{7} - \dfrac{5}{7} =$

④ $3\dfrac{2}{8} - 2\dfrac{5}{8} =$

⑤ $2\dfrac{4}{9} - \dfrac{8}{9} =$

⑥ $3\dfrac{3}{10} - 1\dfrac{6}{10} =$

⑦ $2\dfrac{6}{12} - 1\dfrac{11}{12} =$

8 Reducing Fractions Ⅰ

date ＿＿/＿＿/＿＿　　score ＿＿/100

1 Divide each numerator and denominator by 2 to reduce them. Write the appropriate number in each box below.

5 points per question

① $\dfrac{2}{4} = \dfrac{\boxed{1}}{2}$

② $\dfrac{2}{6} = \dfrac{\boxed{}}{3}$

③ $\dfrac{4}{6} = \dfrac{\boxed{}}{\boxed{}}$

④ $\dfrac{2}{8} = \dfrac{\boxed{}}{\boxed{}}$

Divide each numerator and denominator by 2. $\dfrac{2}{4} = \dfrac{2 \div 2}{4 \div 2} = \dfrac{1}{2}$

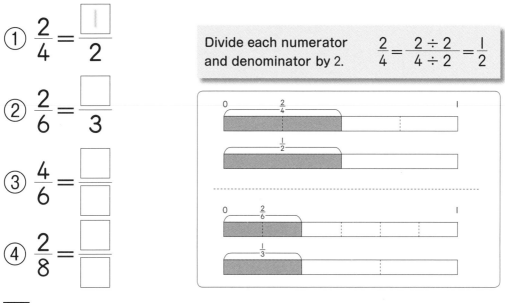

2 Divide each numerator and denominator by 5 to reduce them. Write the appropriate number in each box below.

6 points per question

① $\dfrac{5}{10} = \dfrac{\boxed{1}}{2}$

Divide each numerator and denominator by 5. $\dfrac{5}{10} = \dfrac{5 \div 5}{10 \div 5} = \dfrac{1}{2}$

② $\dfrac{5}{15} = \dfrac{\boxed{}}{3}$

③ $\dfrac{10}{15} = \dfrac{\boxed{}}{\boxed{}}$

④ $\dfrac{5}{20} = \dfrac{\boxed{}}{4}$

⑤ $\dfrac{15}{20} = \dfrac{\boxed{}}{\boxed{}}$

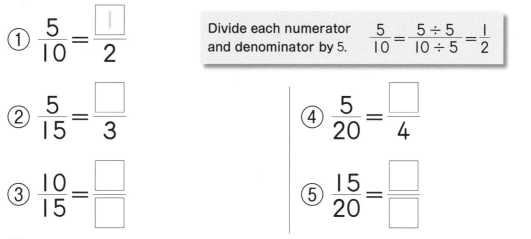

3 Reduce the fractions below by dividing by 2 or 5.

5 points per question

① $\dfrac{2}{6} =$

② $\dfrac{4}{10} =$

③ $\dfrac{5}{10} =$

④ $\dfrac{2}{12} =$

⑤ $\dfrac{10}{12} =$

⑥ $\dfrac{10}{15} =$

⑦ $\dfrac{5}{20} =$

⑧ $\dfrac{14}{24} =$

⑨ $\dfrac{10}{25} =$

⑩ $\dfrac{5}{30} =$

9 Reducing Fractions Ⅱ

date / / score /100

1 Reduce the fractions. Write the appropriate number in each box below.

5 points per question

① $\dfrac{3}{6} = \dfrac{\square}{\square}$

A **factor** is a divisor of a number that leaves no remainders.
When two numbers share the same factor, it is a **common factor**.

What is the common factor of the numerator and the denominator?
The common factor of 3 and 6 is 3, so $\dfrac{3}{6} = \dfrac{3 \div 3}{6 \div 3} = \dfrac{1}{2}$

② $\dfrac{3}{9} = \dfrac{\square}{\square}$

③ $\dfrac{6}{9} = \dfrac{\square}{\square}$

2 Reduce after finding each common factor. Write the appropriate number in each box below.

5 points per question

① The common factor of 6 and 8 is $\boxed{2}$, therefore $\dfrac{6}{8} = \dfrac{\square}{\square}$

② The common factor of 5 and 10 is $\square$, therefore $\dfrac{5}{10} = \dfrac{\square}{\square}$

③ The common factor of 7 and 14 is $\square$, therefore $\dfrac{7}{14} = \dfrac{\square}{\square}$

3 Reduce the fractions below.

① $\dfrac{3}{12} =$

② $\dfrac{2}{14} =$

③ $\dfrac{6}{12} =$

④ $\dfrac{3}{15} =$

⑤ $\dfrac{9}{15} =$

⑥ $\dfrac{5}{15} =$

⑦ $\dfrac{10}{15} =$

⑧ $\dfrac{10}{35} =$

⑨ $\dfrac{21}{35} =$

⑩ $\dfrac{28}{35} =$

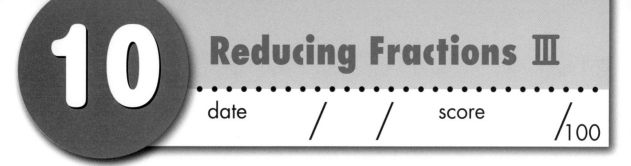

1 Reduce each fraction below by dividing by the Greatest Common Factor (GCF). Write the appropriate number in each box below.

5 points per question

① $\dfrac{4}{8} = \dfrac{\square}{\square}$

> **Greatest Common Factor** (GCF) is the largest common factor of two numbers.

$$\frac{4}{8} = \frac{4 \div 2}{8 \div 2} = \frac{2}{4} \quad \rightarrow \quad \frac{2}{4} = \frac{2 \div 2}{4 \div 2} = \frac{1}{2}$$

It is better to reduce the fraction by using the GCF so you only must reduce it once, as shown below.

$$\frac{4}{8} = \frac{4 \div 4}{8 \div 4} = \frac{1}{2}$$

② $\dfrac{4}{12} = \dfrac{\square}{\square}$

③ $\dfrac{8}{12} = \dfrac{\square}{\square}$

2 Reduce after finding each GCF. Write the appropriate number in each box below.

5 points per question

① The GCF of 6 and 12 is $\boxed{6}$, therefore $\dfrac{6}{12} = \dfrac{\square}{\square}$

② The GCF of 4 and 16 is $\boxed{}$, therefore $\dfrac{4}{16} = \dfrac{\square}{\square}$

③ The GCF of 8 and 20 is $\boxed{}$, therefore $\dfrac{8}{20} = \dfrac{\square}{\square}$

3 Reduce the fractions below.

(4 points per question)

① $\dfrac{8}{16} =$

② $\dfrac{12}{16} =$

③ $\dfrac{6}{18} =$

④ $\dfrac{12}{18} =$

⑤ $\dfrac{4}{20} =$

⑥ $\dfrac{10}{20} =$

⑦ $\dfrac{6}{24} =$

⑧ $\dfrac{8}{24} =$

⑨ $\dfrac{16}{24} =$

⑩ $\dfrac{18}{24} =$

4 Time is represented by fractions below. Write the appropriate number in each box.

(10 points per question)

① 15 minutes $= \dfrac{15}{60}$ hour $= \dfrac{\square}{4}$ hour

└— Divide by 15 —┘

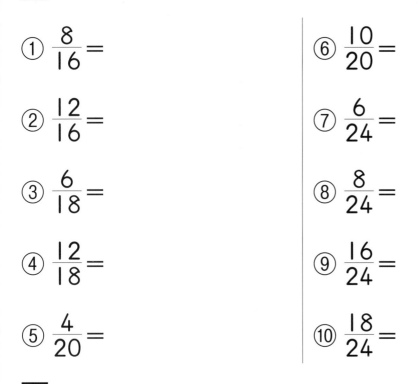

I hour is 60 minutes. So X minutes is $\dfrac{X}{60}$ hour.

② 20 minutes $= \dfrac{\square}{60}$ hour $= \dfrac{\square}{3}$ hour

③ 45 minutes $= \dfrac{\square}{60}$ hour $= \dfrac{\square}{4}$ hour

11 Proportional Fractions

date   /   /   score   /100

1 Make proportional fractions by multiplying the numerator and denominator by the same number. Write the appropriate number in each box below.

(5 points per question)

> If both the numerator and denominator are multiplied by the same number, the value of the fraction doesn't change.

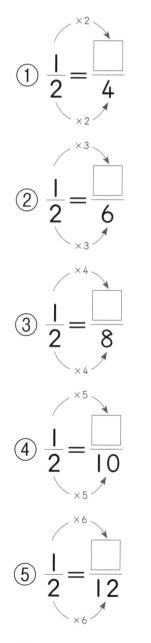

① $\dfrac{1}{2} = \dfrac{\square}{4}$ (×2)

② $\dfrac{1}{2} = \dfrac{\square}{6}$ (×3)

③ $\dfrac{1}{2} = \dfrac{\square}{8}$ (×4)

④ $\dfrac{1}{2} = \dfrac{\square}{10}$ (×5)

⑤ $\dfrac{1}{2} = \dfrac{\square}{12}$ (×6)

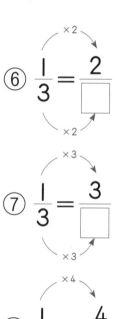

⑥ $\dfrac{1}{3} = \dfrac{2}{\square}$ (×2)

⑦ $\dfrac{1}{3} = \dfrac{3}{\square}$ (×3)

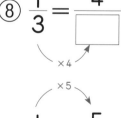

⑧ $\dfrac{1}{3} = \dfrac{4}{\square}$ (×4)

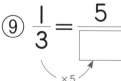

⑨ $\dfrac{1}{3} = \dfrac{5}{\square}$ (×5)

22   ©Kumon Publishing Co., Ltd.

2 Make proportional fractions by multiplying the numerator and denominator by the same number. Write the appropriate number in each box below.

5 points per question

① $\dfrac{2}{3} = \dfrac{\square}{6}$

② $\dfrac{3}{5} = \dfrac{9}{\square}$

③ $\dfrac{2}{4} = \dfrac{\square}{12}$

④ $\dfrac{5}{7} = \dfrac{10}{\square}$

⑤ $\dfrac{4}{5} = \dfrac{\square}{20}$

⑥ $\dfrac{7}{8} = \dfrac{\square}{24}$

⑦ $\dfrac{8}{10} = \dfrac{\square}{50}$

⑧ $\dfrac{4}{6} = \dfrac{\square}{24}$

⑨ $\dfrac{3}{7} = \dfrac{6}{\square}$

⑩ $\dfrac{1}{4} = \dfrac{5}{\square}$

⑪ $\dfrac{6}{9} = \dfrac{24}{\square}$

1 Write the appropriate number in each box below.

① $\dfrac{1}{2} + \dfrac{1}{4} = \dfrac{\Box}{4} + \dfrac{1}{4} = \dfrac{\Box}{4}$ (×2)

> If the denominators are different, make the denominators equal before adding.

② $\dfrac{2}{3} + \dfrac{1}{6} = \dfrac{\Box}{6} + \dfrac{1}{6} = \dfrac{\Box}{6}$

③ $\dfrac{1}{3} + \dfrac{2}{9} = \dfrac{\Box}{9} + \dfrac{2}{9} = \dfrac{\Box}{9}$

④ $\dfrac{1}{8} + \dfrac{1}{4} = \dfrac{1}{8} + \dfrac{\Box}{8} = \dfrac{\Box}{8}$

⑤ $\dfrac{3}{8} + \dfrac{1}{2} = \dfrac{3}{8} + \dfrac{\Box}{8} = \dfrac{\Box}{8}$

> Keep going. Your work will pay off.

⑥ $\dfrac{3}{10} + \dfrac{2}{5} = \dfrac{3}{10} + \dfrac{\Box}{10} = \dfrac{\Box}{10}$

2 Add.

① $\dfrac{1}{4} + \dfrac{3}{8} =$

② $\dfrac{1}{3} + \dfrac{4}{9} =$

③ $\dfrac{1}{5} + \dfrac{1}{10} =$

④ $\dfrac{1}{10} + \dfrac{4}{5} =$

⑤ $\dfrac{1}{2} + \dfrac{1}{12} =$

⑥ $\dfrac{1}{3} + \dfrac{7}{12} =$

⑦ $\dfrac{5}{12} + \dfrac{1}{6} =$

⑧ $\dfrac{3}{5} + \dfrac{4}{15} =$

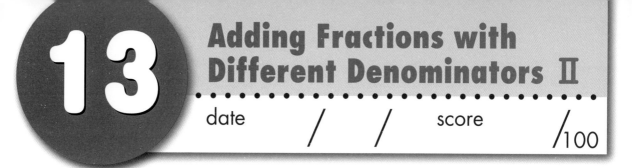
1 Write the appropriate number in each box below.

(6 points per question)

① $\dfrac{1}{2} + \dfrac{1}{3} = \dfrac{\Box}{6} + \dfrac{\Box}{6} = \dfrac{\Box}{6}$

> If the denominators are different, make the denominators equal before adding.
> The multiples of 2 are 2, 4, ⑥, ⋯ ⎫ The **Least Common Multiple** (LCM) of 2 and
> The multiples of 3 are 3, ⑥, 9, ⋯ ⎭ 3 is 6.

② $\dfrac{2}{3} + \dfrac{1}{4} = \dfrac{\Box}{12} + \dfrac{\Box}{12} = \dfrac{\Box}{12}$

③ $\dfrac{1}{5} + \dfrac{3}{4} = \dfrac{\Box}{20} + \dfrac{\Box}{20} = \dfrac{\Box}{20}$

The **Least Common Denominator** (LCD) is the smallest number that can be used as the denominator of two or more fractions in a number sentence. The LCD is the same as the Least Common Multiple of the denominators.

④ $\dfrac{2}{5} + \dfrac{1}{3} = \dfrac{\Box}{15} + \dfrac{\Box}{15} = \dfrac{\Box}{15}$

⑤ $\dfrac{1}{6} + \dfrac{3}{5} = \dfrac{\Box}{30} + \dfrac{\Box}{30} = \dfrac{\Box}{30}$

⑥ $\dfrac{2}{5} + \dfrac{1}{2} = \dfrac{\Box}{10} + \dfrac{\Box}{10} = \dfrac{\Box}{10}$

2 Add.

8 points per question

① $\dfrac{3}{5} + \dfrac{1}{4} =$

② $\dfrac{1}{3} + \dfrac{4}{7} =$

③ $\dfrac{1}{8} + \dfrac{2}{3} =$

④ $\dfrac{1}{3} + \dfrac{3}{10} =$

⑤ $\dfrac{2}{7} + \dfrac{3}{5} =$

⑥ $\dfrac{2}{9} + \dfrac{3}{4} =$

⑦ $\dfrac{5}{7} + \dfrac{1}{6} =$

⑧ $\dfrac{1}{5} + \dfrac{4}{9} =$

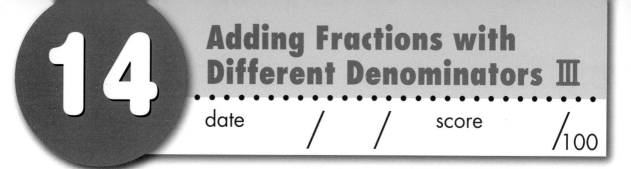

1 Find the Least Common Denominator, and then add. Write the appropriate number in each box below.

5 points per question

① $\dfrac{1}{4} + \dfrac{1}{6} = \dfrac{\boxed{}}{12} + \dfrac{\boxed{}}{12} = \dfrac{\boxed{}}{12}$

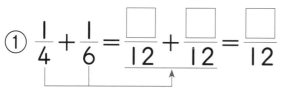

The Least Common Multiple of 4 and 6 is 12.

You can calculate $\dfrac{1}{4} + \dfrac{1}{6} = \dfrac{6}{24} + \dfrac{4}{24} = \dfrac{10}{24} = \dfrac{5}{12}$ by multiplying the denominators. However, it is easier to calculate $\dfrac{1}{4} + \dfrac{1}{6} = \dfrac{3}{12} + \dfrac{2}{12} = \dfrac{5}{12}$ by using the Least Common Multiple.

Find the Least Common Multiple of the denominators;

The multiples of 4 are: 4, 8, ⑫, ···

The multiples of 6 are: 6, ⑫, 18, ···

Choose the Least Common Multiple of 4 and 6.

② The Least Common Multiple of 4 and 10 is 20.

$\dfrac{3}{4} + \dfrac{1}{10} = \dfrac{\boxed{}}{20} + \dfrac{\boxed{}}{20} = \dfrac{\boxed{}}{20}$

You can find the Least Common Multiple by first listing the multiples of the larger number. Then find the lowest multiple that can be divided by the smaller number.

③ The Least Common Multiple of 8 and 6 is 24.

$\dfrac{1}{8} + \dfrac{5}{6} = \dfrac{\boxed{}}{24} + \dfrac{\boxed{}}{24} = \dfrac{\boxed{}}{24}$

④ The Least Common Multiple of 12 and 8 is 24.

$\dfrac{5}{12} + \dfrac{3}{8} = \dfrac{\boxed{}}{24} + \dfrac{\boxed{}}{24} = \dfrac{\boxed{}}{24}$

2 Add.

① $\dfrac{3}{4} + \dfrac{1}{6} =$

② $\dfrac{1}{6} + \dfrac{2}{9} =$

③ $\dfrac{4}{9} + \dfrac{1}{6} =$

④ $\dfrac{3}{10} + \dfrac{1}{4} =$

⑤ $\dfrac{1}{8} + \dfrac{1}{6} =$

⑥ $\dfrac{1}{6} + \dfrac{3}{8} =$

⑦ $\dfrac{3}{8} + \dfrac{1}{12} =$

⑧ $\dfrac{1}{9} + \dfrac{1}{12} =$

1 Write the appropriate number in each box below.

4 points per question

① $\dfrac{5}{6} + \dfrac{1}{10} = \dfrac{\Box}{30} + \dfrac{\Box}{30} = \dfrac{\Box}{30} = \dfrac{\Box}{15}$

Find the Least Common Denominator.   Reduce it.

If the answer can be reduced, reduce it!

② $\dfrac{1}{2} + \dfrac{1}{6} = \dfrac{\Box}{6} + \dfrac{1}{6} = \dfrac{\Box}{6} = \dfrac{\Box}{3}$

Find the Least Common Denominator.   Reduce it.

③ $\dfrac{1}{12} + \dfrac{2}{3} = \dfrac{1}{12} + \dfrac{\Box}{12} = \dfrac{\Box}{12} = \dfrac{\Box}{4}$

Find the Least Common Denominator.   Reduce it.

④ $\dfrac{1}{4} + \dfrac{1}{6} = \dfrac{\Box}{12} + \dfrac{\Box}{12} = \dfrac{\Box}{12}$

Good job!

⑤ $\dfrac{7}{20} + \dfrac{2}{5} = \dfrac{7}{20} + \dfrac{\Box}{20} = \dfrac{\Box}{20} = \dfrac{\Box}{4}$

2 Add.

① $\dfrac{1}{5} + \dfrac{3}{10} =$

② $\dfrac{1}{3} + \dfrac{5}{12} =$

③ $\dfrac{5}{12} + \dfrac{1}{4} =$

④ $\dfrac{5}{18} + \dfrac{2}{9} =$

⑤ $\dfrac{3}{20} + \dfrac{1}{4} =$

⑥ $\dfrac{1}{5} + \dfrac{1}{20} =$

⑦ $\dfrac{1}{10} + \dfrac{11}{15} =$

⑧ $\dfrac{1}{6} + \dfrac{1}{10} =$

16 Adding Fractions with Different Denominators V

date   /   /   score   /100

1 Write the appropriate number in each box below.

[5 points per question]

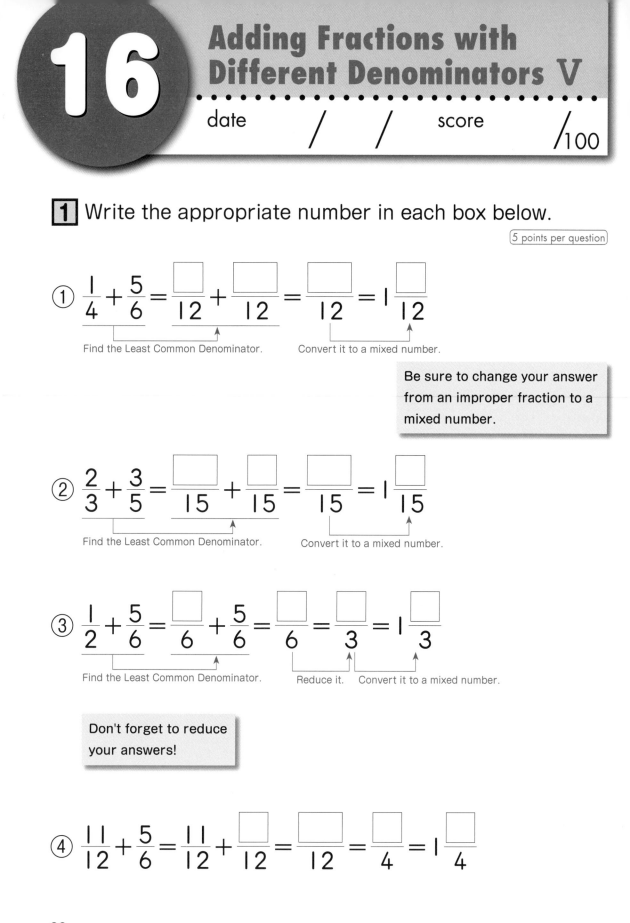

① $\dfrac{1}{4} + \dfrac{5}{6} = \dfrac{\square}{12} + \dfrac{\square}{12} = \dfrac{\square}{12} = 1\dfrac{\square}{12}$

Find the Least Common Denominator.   Convert it to a mixed number.

Be sure to change your answer from an improper fraction to a mixed number.

② $\dfrac{2}{3} + \dfrac{3}{5} = \dfrac{\square}{15} + \dfrac{\square}{15} = \dfrac{\square}{15} = 1\dfrac{\square}{15}$

Find the Least Common Denominator.   Convert it to a mixed number.

③ $\dfrac{1}{2} + \dfrac{5}{6} = \dfrac{\square}{6} + \dfrac{5}{6} = \dfrac{\square}{6} = \dfrac{\square}{3} = 1\dfrac{\square}{3}$

Find the Least Common Denominator.   Reduce it.   Convert it to a mixed number.

Don't forget to reduce your answers!

④ $\dfrac{11}{12} + \dfrac{5}{6} = \dfrac{11}{12} + \dfrac{\square}{12} = \dfrac{\square}{12} = \dfrac{\square}{4} = 1\dfrac{\square}{4}$

2 Add.

① $\dfrac{2}{3} + \dfrac{1}{2} =$

② $\dfrac{3}{4} + \dfrac{5}{8} =$

③ $\dfrac{3}{4} + \dfrac{1}{3} =$

④ $\dfrac{4}{5} + \dfrac{1}{4} =$

⑤ $\dfrac{2}{3} + \dfrac{5}{6} =$

⑥ $\dfrac{3}{4} + \dfrac{7}{20} =$

⑦ $\dfrac{3}{10} + \dfrac{5}{6} =$

⑧ $\dfrac{13}{15} + \dfrac{1}{3} =$

1 Write the appropriate number in each box below.

5 points per question

① $1\dfrac{1}{2}+2\dfrac{1}{3}=1\dfrac{\square}{6}+2\dfrac{\square}{6}=3\dfrac{\square}{6}$

Find the Least Common Denominator.

② $1\dfrac{1}{4}+1\dfrac{3}{5}=1\dfrac{\square}{20}+1\dfrac{\square}{20}=2\dfrac{\square}{20}$

③ $1\dfrac{1}{6}+2\dfrac{1}{3}=1\dfrac{1}{6}+2\dfrac{\square}{6}=3\dfrac{\square}{6}=3\dfrac{\square}{2}$

Reduce it.

Don't forget to reduce your answers!

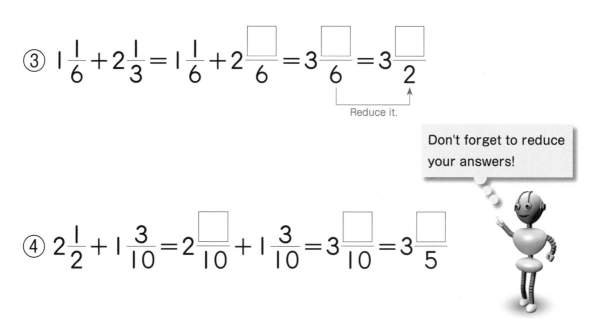

④ $2\dfrac{1}{2}+1\dfrac{3}{10}=2\dfrac{\square}{10}+1\dfrac{3}{10}=3\dfrac{\square}{10}=3\dfrac{\square}{5}$

2 Add the mixed numbers below.

① $3\frac{1}{4} + 2\frac{1}{2} =$

② $1\frac{1}{2} + 1\frac{2}{5} =$

③ $2\frac{1}{4} + 1\frac{2}{3} =$

④ $1\frac{3}{4} + 3\frac{1}{6} =$

⑤ $1\frac{2}{5} + 2\frac{1}{10} =$

⑥ $2\frac{1}{12} + 2\frac{3}{4} =$

⑦ $1\frac{1}{3} + 1\frac{1}{15} =$

⑧ $1\frac{8}{21} + 2\frac{2}{7} =$

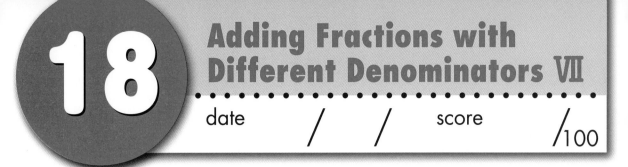
1 Write the appropriate number in each box below.

(10 points per question)

① $1\dfrac{1}{3} + 2\dfrac{3}{4} = 1\dfrac{\boxed{}}{12} + 2\dfrac{\boxed{}}{12} = 3\dfrac{\boxed{}}{12} = 4\dfrac{\boxed{}}{12}$

② $1\dfrac{1}{2} + 2\dfrac{2}{3} = 1\dfrac{\boxed{}}{6} + 2\dfrac{\boxed{}}{6} = 3\dfrac{\boxed{}}{6} = 4\dfrac{\boxed{}}{6}$

③ $1\dfrac{7}{15} + \dfrac{5}{6} = 1\dfrac{\boxed{}}{30} + \dfrac{\boxed{}}{30} = 1\dfrac{\boxed{}}{30} = 1\dfrac{\boxed{}}{10} = 2\dfrac{\boxed{}}{10}$

Don't forget to reduce if you can, like so: $1\dfrac{39}{30} = 2\dfrac{9}{30} = 2\dfrac{3}{10}$.

2 Add.

① $1\dfrac{1}{2}+\dfrac{5}{8}=$

② $\dfrac{3}{4}+3\dfrac{2}{5}=$

③ $\dfrac{2}{3}+3\dfrac{3}{8}=$

④ $3\dfrac{5}{6}+1\dfrac{7}{9}=$

⑤ $3\dfrac{2}{3}+\dfrac{5}{6}=$

⑥ $2\dfrac{1}{2}+\dfrac{7}{10}=$

⑦ $2\dfrac{3}{4}+1\dfrac{5}{12}=$

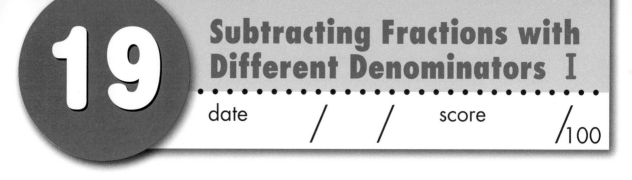

19 Subtracting Fractions with Different Denominators I

date　　／　／　　score　／100

1 Write the appropriate number in each box below.

5 points per question

① $\dfrac{1}{2} - \dfrac{1}{4} = \dfrac{\square}{4} - \dfrac{1}{4} = \dfrac{\square}{4}$

> When the denominators are different, make the denominators equal before subtracting.

② $\dfrac{1}{4} - \dfrac{1}{8} = \dfrac{\square}{8} - \dfrac{1}{8} = \dfrac{\square}{8}$

③ $\dfrac{5}{6} - \dfrac{2}{3} = \dfrac{5}{6} - \dfrac{\square}{6} = \dfrac{\square}{6}$

④ $\dfrac{4}{5} - \dfrac{1}{10} = \dfrac{\square}{10} - \dfrac{1}{10} = \dfrac{\square}{10}$

⑤ $\dfrac{4}{9} - \dfrac{1}{3} = \dfrac{4}{9} - \dfrac{\square}{9} = \dfrac{\square}{9}$

⑥ $\dfrac{5}{6} - \dfrac{5}{12} = \dfrac{\square}{12} - \dfrac{5}{12} = \dfrac{\square}{12}$

2 Subtract.

① $\dfrac{1}{3} - \dfrac{1}{6} =$

② $\dfrac{1}{2} - \dfrac{1}{8} =$

③ $\dfrac{1}{2} - \dfrac{3}{8} =$

④ $\dfrac{3}{4} - \dfrac{3}{8} =$

⑤ $\dfrac{1}{3} - \dfrac{1}{9} =$

⑥ $\dfrac{2}{3} - \dfrac{2}{9} =$

⑦ $\dfrac{2}{3} - \dfrac{1}{10} =$

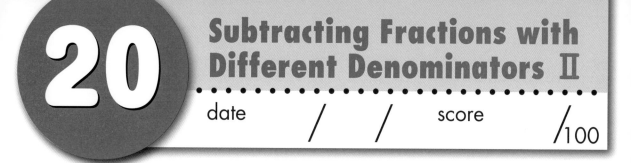

Subtracting Fractions with Different Denominators II

date / / score /100

1 Find the Least Common Denominator, and then subtract. Write the appropriate number in each box below.

5 points per question

① $\dfrac{1}{2} - \dfrac{2}{5} = \dfrac{\boxed{}}{10} - \dfrac{\boxed{}}{10} = \dfrac{\boxed{}}{10}$

The Least Common Multiple of 2 and 5 is 10, therefore 10 is the Least Common Denominator.

② $\dfrac{3}{4} - \dfrac{1}{6} = \dfrac{\boxed{}}{12} - \dfrac{\boxed{}}{12} = \dfrac{\boxed{}}{12}$

The Least Common Multiple of 4 and 6 is 12, therefore 12 is the Least Common Denominator.

③ $\dfrac{2}{3} - \dfrac{1}{5} = \dfrac{\boxed{}}{15} - \dfrac{\boxed{}}{15} = \dfrac{\boxed{}}{15}$

④ $\dfrac{5}{8} - \dfrac{1}{6} = \dfrac{\boxed{}}{24} - \dfrac{\boxed{}}{24} = \dfrac{\boxed{}}{24}$

⑤ $\dfrac{8}{9} - \dfrac{5}{6} = \dfrac{\boxed{}}{18} - \dfrac{\boxed{}}{18} = \dfrac{\boxed{}}{18}$

⑥ $\dfrac{7}{6} - \dfrac{2}{5} = \dfrac{\boxed{}}{30} - \dfrac{\boxed{}}{30} = \dfrac{\boxed{}}{30}$

2 Subtract.

① $\dfrac{1}{2} - \dfrac{1}{5} =$

② $\dfrac{4}{5} - \dfrac{1}{2} =$

③ $\dfrac{3}{5} - \dfrac{1}{3} =$

④ $\dfrac{1}{3} - \dfrac{1}{5} =$

⑤ $\dfrac{1}{4} - \dfrac{1}{5} =$

⑥ $\dfrac{5}{4} - \dfrac{1}{3} =$

⑦ $\dfrac{10}{9} - \dfrac{5}{6} =$

1 Write the appropriate number in each box below.

5 points per question

① $\dfrac{2}{3} - \dfrac{1}{6} = \dfrac{\square}{6} - \dfrac{1}{6} = \dfrac{\square}{6} = \dfrac{\square}{2}$

Find the Least Common Denominator.　Reduce it.

Don't forget to reduce your answer.

② $\dfrac{5}{6} - \dfrac{1}{2} = \dfrac{5}{6} - \dfrac{\square}{6} = \dfrac{\square}{6} = \dfrac{\square}{3}$

Find the Least Common Denominator.　Reduce it.

③ $\dfrac{9}{10} - \dfrac{5}{6} = \dfrac{\square}{30} - \dfrac{\square}{30} = \dfrac{\square}{30} = \dfrac{\square}{15}$

④ $\dfrac{1}{2} - \dfrac{1}{6} = \dfrac{\square}{6} - \dfrac{1}{6} = \dfrac{\square}{6} = \dfrac{\square}{3}$

⑤ $\dfrac{6}{5} - \dfrac{7}{10} = \dfrac{\square}{10} - \dfrac{7}{10} = \dfrac{\square}{10} = \dfrac{\square}{2}$

⑥ $\dfrac{13}{12} - \dfrac{1}{4} = \dfrac{13}{12} - \dfrac{\square}{12} = \dfrac{\square}{12} = \dfrac{\square}{6}$

2 Subtract.

① $\dfrac{1}{2} - \dfrac{1}{10} =$

② $\dfrac{4}{5} - \dfrac{3}{10} =$

③ $\dfrac{7}{10} - \dfrac{1}{5} =$

④ $\dfrac{11}{10} - \dfrac{3}{5} =$

⑤ $\dfrac{14}{15} - \dfrac{1}{3} =$

⑥ $\dfrac{7}{20} - \dfrac{1}{4} =$

⑦ $\dfrac{7}{6} - \dfrac{7}{10} =$

1 Write the appropriate number in each box below.

10 points per question

① $2\dfrac{1}{2} - 1\dfrac{1}{3} = 2\dfrac{\square}{6} - 1\dfrac{\square}{6}$

Find the Least Common Denominator.

$= 1\dfrac{\square}{6}$

Subtract each part separately—subtract the whole numbers, and then subtract the fractions.

② $2\dfrac{2}{3} - 1\dfrac{1}{6} = 2\dfrac{\square}{6} - 1\dfrac{1}{6}$

Find the Least Common Denominator.

$= 1\dfrac{\square}{6} = 1\dfrac{\square}{2}$

Reduce it.

Don't forget to reduce your answer.

③ $3\dfrac{5}{9} - 2\dfrac{1}{6} = 3\dfrac{\square}{18} - 2\dfrac{\square}{18}$

$= 1\dfrac{\square}{18}$

2 Subtract.

① $3\dfrac{5}{6} - 1\dfrac{1}{3} =$

② $3\dfrac{1}{3} - 1\dfrac{2}{9} =$

③ $2\dfrac{1}{2} - 1\dfrac{3}{10} =$

④ $4\dfrac{7}{10} - 2\dfrac{1}{2} =$

⑤ $3\dfrac{1}{4} - 1\dfrac{1}{10} =$

⑥ $2\dfrac{5}{6} - 1\dfrac{1}{8} =$

⑦ $2\dfrac{3}{4} - 1\dfrac{5}{7} =$

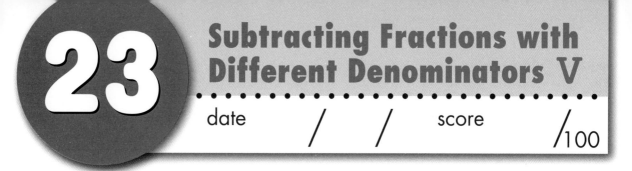

1 Write the appropriate number in each box below.

10 points per question

① $3\frac{1}{2} - 1\frac{2}{3} = 3\frac{\boxed{}}{6} - 1\frac{\boxed{}}{6} = 2\frac{\boxed{}}{6} - 1\frac{\boxed{}}{6} = 1\frac{5}{6}$

② $1\frac{1}{5} - \frac{5}{6} = 1\frac{\boxed{}}{30} - \frac{\boxed{}}{30} = \frac{\boxed{}}{30} - \frac{\boxed{}}{30} = \frac{\boxed{}}{30}$

③ $4\frac{1}{6} - 2\frac{2}{3} = 4\frac{1}{6} - 2\frac{\boxed{}}{6}$

$= 3\frac{\boxed{}}{6} - 2\frac{\boxed{}}{6}$

$= 1\frac{\boxed{}}{6} = 1\frac{\boxed{}}{2}$

You're doing great!

2 Subtract.

① $2\dfrac{1}{3} - \dfrac{7}{9} =$

② $3\dfrac{2}{15} - 1\dfrac{3}{5} =$

③ $2\dfrac{1}{4} - 1\dfrac{2}{3} =$

④ $3\dfrac{1}{6} - \dfrac{5}{8} =$

⑤ $3\dfrac{2}{15} - 1\dfrac{4}{5} =$

⑥ $5\dfrac{1}{2} - 2\dfrac{5}{6} =$

⑦ $2\dfrac{1}{10} - \dfrac{5}{6} =$

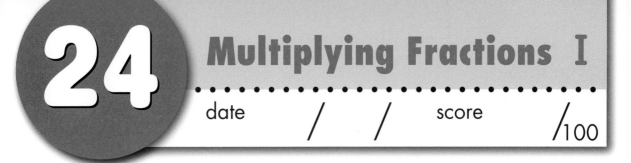

Multiplying Fractions I

date / / score /100

1 Write the appropriate number in each box below.

5 points per question

① $\dfrac{2}{7} \times 3 = \dfrac{2}{7} \times \dfrac{3}{1} = \dfrac{\square}{7}$

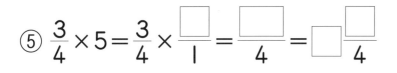

To multiply a whole number and a fraction, multiply the numerator by the whole number and keep the denominator, as shown.

② $\dfrac{1}{7} \times 9 = \dfrac{1}{7} \times \dfrac{\square}{1} = \dfrac{\square}{7} = \square\dfrac{\square}{7}$

③ $\dfrac{4}{9} \times 2 = \dfrac{4}{9} \times \dfrac{\square}{1} = \dfrac{\square}{9}$

④ $\dfrac{1}{3} \times 7 = \dfrac{1}{3} \times \dfrac{\square}{1} = \dfrac{\square}{3} = \square\dfrac{\square}{3}$

⑤ $\dfrac{3}{4} \times 5 = \dfrac{3}{4} \times \dfrac{\square}{1} = \dfrac{\square}{4} = \square\dfrac{\square}{4}$

⑥ $\dfrac{2}{11} \times 4 = \dfrac{2}{11} \times \dfrac{\square}{1} = \dfrac{\square}{11}$

2 Multiply.

(7 points per question)

① $\frac{1}{2} \times 5 =$

② $\frac{3}{5} \times 2 =$

③ $\frac{2}{7} \times 3 =$

④ $\frac{3}{10} \times 7 =$

⑤ $\frac{1}{4} \times 9 =$

⑥ $\frac{1}{6} \times 7 =$

⑦ $\frac{3}{8} \times 3 =$

⑧ $\frac{2}{3} \times 4 =$

⑨ $\frac{3}{11} \times 6 =$

⑩ $\frac{1}{5} \times 8 =$

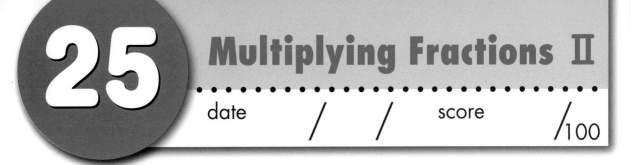
1 Write the appropriate number in each box below.

10 points per question

① $\dfrac{5}{12} \times 2 = \dfrac{5}{12} \times \dfrac{2}{1} = \dfrac{\square}{\square}$

with boxes above and below

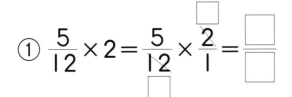

> If you can, reduce the numbers before multiplying, so you don't have to reduce your final answer.

↓

$$\frac{5}{12} \times 2 = \frac{5}{12} \times \frac{2}{1}$$
$$= \frac{10}{12}$$
$$= \frac{5}{6}$$

$$\frac{5}{12} \times 2 = \frac{5}{\underset{6}{12}} \times \frac{\overset{1}{2}}{1}$$
$$= \frac{5}{6}$$

It is more efficient to reduce the numbers before multiplying, as shown on the right.

② $\dfrac{7}{8} \times 4 = \dfrac{7}{8} \times \dfrac{4}{1} = \dfrac{\square}{\square} = \square\dfrac{\square}{2}$

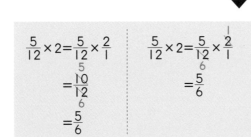

③ $\dfrac{8}{15} \times 3 = \dfrac{8}{15} \times \dfrac{3}{1} = \dfrac{\square}{\square} = \square\dfrac{\square}{5}$

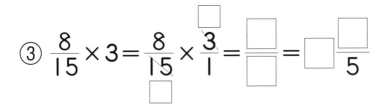

2 Multiply.

① $\dfrac{5}{6} \times 3 =$

② $\dfrac{9}{20} \times 4 =$

③ $\dfrac{11}{25} \times 5 =$

④ $\dfrac{7}{10} \times 6 =$

⑤ $\dfrac{17}{36} \times 8 =$

⑥ $\dfrac{2}{35} \times 7 =$

⑦ $\dfrac{1}{18} \times 10 =$

⑧ $\dfrac{3}{16} \times 2 =$

⑨ $\dfrac{13}{30} \times 9 =$

⑩ $\dfrac{23}{24} \times 12 =$

1 Write the appropriate number in each box below.

5 points per question

① $\dfrac{5}{7} \div 2 = \dfrac{5}{7} \div \dfrac{\boxed{2}}{1} = \dfrac{5}{7} \times \dfrac{1}{\boxed{2}} = \dfrac{5}{\boxed{14}}$

> To divide a whole number by a fraction, first convert the whole number to a fraction. Then, turn the second fraction upside-down and multiply the numerators and denominators separately.

② $\dfrac{1}{4} \div 5 = \dfrac{1}{4} \div \dfrac{\boxed{}}{1} = \dfrac{1}{4} \times \dfrac{1}{\boxed{}} = \dfrac{1}{\boxed{}}$

③ $\dfrac{3}{8} \div 7 = \dfrac{3}{8} \div \dfrac{\boxed{}}{1} = \dfrac{3}{8} \times \dfrac{1}{\boxed{}} = \dfrac{3}{\boxed{}}$

④ $\dfrac{2}{3} \div 9 = \dfrac{2}{3} \div \dfrac{\boxed{}}{1} = \dfrac{2}{3} \times \dfrac{1}{\boxed{}} = \dfrac{2}{\boxed{}}$

⑤ $\dfrac{4}{5} \div 3 = \dfrac{4}{5} \div \dfrac{\boxed{}}{1} = \dfrac{4}{5} \times \dfrac{1}{\boxed{}} = \dfrac{4}{\boxed{}}$

⑥ $\dfrac{1}{2} \div 4 = \dfrac{1}{2} \div \dfrac{\boxed{}}{1} = \dfrac{1}{2} \times \dfrac{1}{\boxed{}} = \dfrac{1}{\boxed{}}$

2 Divide.

① $\dfrac{5}{6} \div 3 =$

② $\dfrac{1}{3} \div 5 =$

③ $\dfrac{2}{5} \div 9 =$

④ $\dfrac{7}{8} \div 2 =$

⑤ $\dfrac{1}{5} \div 7 =$

⑥ $\dfrac{3}{7} \div 4 =$

⑦ $\dfrac{7}{9} \div 8 =$

⑧ $\dfrac{3}{7} \div 7 =$

⑨ $\dfrac{1}{10} \div 6 =$

⑩ $\dfrac{2}{7} \div 5 =$

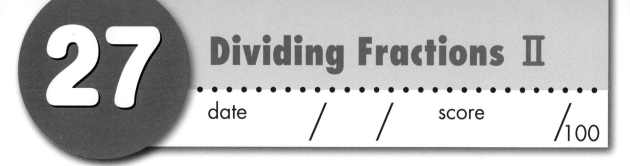

27 Dividing Fractions II

date / / score /100

1 Write the appropriate number in each box below.

6 points per question

① $\dfrac{6}{7} \div 2 = \dfrac{6}{7} \div \dfrac{2}{1} = \dfrac{6}{7} \times \dfrac{1}{2} = \dfrac{\Box}{\Box}$

Don't forget to reduce before multiplying.

② $\dfrac{3}{4} \div 6 = \dfrac{3}{4} \div \dfrac{6}{1} = \dfrac{3}{4} \times \dfrac{1}{6} = \dfrac{\Box}{\Box}$

③ $\dfrac{5}{8} \div 5 = \dfrac{5}{8} \div \dfrac{5}{1} = \dfrac{5}{8} \times \dfrac{1}{5} = \dfrac{\Box}{\Box}$

④ $\dfrac{9}{10} \div 3 = \dfrac{9}{10} \div \dfrac{3}{1} = \dfrac{9}{10} \times \dfrac{1}{3} = \dfrac{\Box}{\Box}$

⑤ $\dfrac{8}{11} \div 2 = \dfrac{8}{11} \div \dfrac{2}{1} = \dfrac{8}{11} \times \dfrac{1}{2} = \dfrac{\Box}{\Box}$

54 ©Kumon Publishing Co., Ltd.

 **Divide.**

7 points per question

① $\dfrac{5}{6} \div 20 =$

② $\dfrac{2}{3} \div 8 =$

③ $\dfrac{4}{5} \div 12 =$

④ $\dfrac{5}{9} \div 15 =$

⑤ $\dfrac{7}{10} \div 14 =$

⑥ $\dfrac{11}{12} \div 22 =$

⑦ $\dfrac{7}{15} \div 7 =$

⑧ $\dfrac{9}{16} \div 6 =$

⑨ $\dfrac{3}{20} \div 9 =$

⑩ $\dfrac{5}{18} \div 10 =$

date   /   /   score   /100

1 Reduce the fractions below.

5 points per question

① $\dfrac{12}{16} =$

② $\dfrac{15}{18} =$

③ $\dfrac{8}{24} =$

④ $\dfrac{14}{35} =$

2 Add.

6 points per question

① $\dfrac{5}{7} + \dfrac{3}{7} =$

② $1\dfrac{2}{5} + 1\dfrac{4}{5} =$

③ $\dfrac{1}{3} + \dfrac{2}{5} =$

④ $\dfrac{3}{4} + \dfrac{5}{6} =$

⑤ $1\dfrac{7}{10} + \dfrac{5}{6} =$